THE
PARADISE MYTH

THE
PARADISE MYTH

JOHN ARMSTRONG

LONDON
OXFORD UNIVERSITY PRESS
NEW YORK TORONTO
1969

Oxford University Press, Ely House, London W. 1

GLASGOW NEW YORK TORONTO MELBOURNE WELLINGTON
CAPE TOWN SALISBURY IBADAN NAIROBI LUSAKA ADDIS ABABA
BOMBAY CALCUTTA MADRAS KARACHI LAHORE DACCA
KUALA LUMPUR SINGAPORE HONG KONG TOKYO

81064

PREFACE

IN writing this study my principal aim has been to make the main ideas and their connections as clear as possible, while trying to keep them subordinate to the particular forms where they find true realization, those works of art which are their proper mode of expression. This purpose will be best served, I believe, for reasons which are embedded in the argument itself, by considering selected groups of material, rather than by a more comprehensive kind of survey. I have sought out liaisons between literature and art from a conviction that imaginative productions in different media can light up important aspects of one another and that the study of literature and the criticism of art constantly need each other's help.

Aware of an inestimable debt to specialists in fields into which I have trespassed, I ask their tolerance if the pursuit of so wide a theme has almost inevitably led to less than exemplary performance within their spheres of interest. Inaccuracy on the basis of present knowledge I have tried to avoid. In principle, an enterprise of the kind undertaken here seems to need no apology, for we cannot seriously want particular specialisms and periods to become so isolated as to be no longer of legitimate interest or profit to those who have not spent a decade or so in mastering their minutiae. It should be added that what follows did not originate in a wish to ride into the modern world a particular theory or set of ideas about ancient literature and art; rather, the relevance of these earlier productions was borne in upon me as a result of the critical interpretations put forward in the second part of this book having assumed something very like their present form.

My warm thanks are due to the Warden and Fellows of Merton College, Oxford, whose kindness and hospitality during a sabbatical term made it possible to give a spell of uninterrupted thought to the problems discussed here. I am most grateful to Professor J. Barr of the Department of Semitic Languages, Manchester University,

The Paradise Myth

for reading the manuscript at an early stage, and for encouraging me to believe that this book, although no contribution to biblical scholarship, might not affront it. I must also thank Professor O. R. Gurney of the Oriental Institute, Oxford University, for kindly giving indispensable guidance, when I first began to concern myself with Sumero-Babylonian literature, and for contributing a number of amendments to the final draft. Likewise, I am indebted to Dr. J. Boardman of the Department of Classical Archaeology, Oxford University, for generously reading the section on hero-reliefs and suggesting several improvements in point of accuracy. I also wish to thank Mrs. T. Dunningham, Mrs. R. Foulks, and Mrs. H. Hills Spedding for skilfully deciphering and typing the manuscript. My greatest debt is to the pupils with whom the main ideas developed here were first hammered out, particularly to Mr. J. C. Keith and Mr. R. G. Massey, who gave invaluable help and encouragement during the first phase of composition.

J. H. S. A.

CONTENTS

PREFACE   *page* v

ILLUSTRATIONS   ix

ACKNOWLEDGEMENTS   x

ABBREVIATIONS   xi

PART ONE
THE PROBLEM

1. INTRODUCTORY   3

2. THEMES IN SUMERIAN AND GREEK MYTH AND
   VISUAL IMAGERY   8
   I. Genesis and Sumerian myth   8
   II. Tree and Snake in Sumerian and Greek myth   15
   III. Tree and Snake in Sumerian and Greek visual imagery   21
   IV. Tree and Snake on Greek hero-reliefs   25

PART TWO
TOWARDS AN INTERPRETATION

3. THEMES IN RENAISSANCE ART AND LITERATURE   39
   I. *Primavera*   39
   II. Shakespeare's Final Period   43
      A. *Antony and Cleopatra*   44
      B. *The Winter's Tale*   60
      C. *The Tempest*   77
   III. *La Tempesta*   98

4. PARADISE LOST   104

5. COLERIDGE: THE ANCIENT MARINER AND KUBLA
   KHAN   124

INDEX   149

ILLUSTRATIONS

1. Athenian Hydria, *c.* 410 B.C., by the Meidias Painter
   (British Museum)   *facing page* 18

2. Libation Vase of Gudea, *c.* 2150 B.C. (Paris, Louvre) [*colour*]   20

3. *a.* Stele of Gudea, *c.* 2150 B.C. (Berlin, Vorderasiatisches
   Museum)   22

   b. Seal of Gudea   22

4. The snake-encircled tree:

   a. Fourth-century Thyrean relief (Athens, National
   Museum)   26

   b. Hellenistic relief from Pergamon (Istanbul, Archaeological Museum)   26

   c. Fourth-century relief from Piraeus (Athens, National
   Museum)   27

   d. Hellenistic relief from Samos (Samos Museum)   27

5. Botticelli: *Primavera* (Florence, Uffizi Gallery)   40

   a. Mercury, from *Primavera*   41

   b. Caduceus of Mercury, and band of cloud, from *Primavera*   41

6. *a.* Botticelli: *The Birth of Venus* (Florence, Uffizi Gallery)   44

   b. Venus goes to the Lover's aid: fifteenth-century MS. of
   Roman de la Rose (Bodleian Library)   44

7. *a.* The Castle of Jealousy: fifteenth-century MS. of Roman
   de la Rose (Bodleian Library)   45

   b. Venus surprises the Castle of Jealousy: fifteenth-century
   MS. of Roman de la Rose (Bodleian Library)   45

8. Giorgione: *La Tempesta* (Venice, Accademia) [*colour*]   98

9. Teniers after Giorgione: *The Finding of Paris* (formerly
   Florence, Loeser Collection)   100

10. Bellini: *Sacred Allegory* (Florence, Uffizi Gallery)   101

ACKNOWLEDGEMENTS

THE translation on pp. 96–7 of *The Spirit Ariel* by R. M. Rilke is by J. B. Leishman and is quoted from his *Selected Poems* of Rilke, by permission of St. John's College, Oxford, and the Hogarth Press, London, and New Directions, Inc., New York. The translated extracts on pp. 15–16 from *Gilgamesh and the Huluppu-Tree*, by S. N. Kramer, are quoted by permission of the Oriental Institute of the University of Chicago; and that on pp. 19–20 from *The Argonautica* of Apollonius Rhodius is from the translation by E. V. Rieu in the Penguin Classics (1959) and is used by permission of Penguin Books Ltd. A shorter version of Chapter 5, section III, appeared in the *Observer*, 21 November 1965.

Plate 3*a*, which previously appeared in *Sumer* by André Patrro (Paris, Gallimard), is reproduced by permission of Bildarchiv Foto Marburg, Marburg/Lahn, Germany, and Plate 3*b* from *Cylinder Seals* by H. Frankfort, by permission of Messrs. Macmillan & Co. Ltd., London.

Thanks are due to the respective museums, galleries, and library mentioned in the captions for permission to reproduce the other plates, and, where not otherwise specified, for providing photographs; also to the following for photographs: Plate 2, M. Chuzeville, Paris; Plate 4*d*, Deutsches Archäologisches Institut, Athens; Plates 5 and 10, Bazzechi, Florence; Plate 6*a*, Mansell Collection, London; Plate 8, Scala Istituto Fotografico Editoriale, Florence; for Plate 9, which is in private ownership, thanks are due to Messrs. Thos. Agnew & Sons, Ltd., London, for a photograph, which is reproduced by their permission.

ABBREVIATIONS

A.N.E.T.	*Ancient Near Eastern Texts relating to the Old Testament*, edited by J. Pritchard (second edition, 1955).
Ath. Mitt.	*Athenische Mitteilungen.*
C.L.	*Collected Letters of Samuel Taylor Coleridge*, edited by E. L. Griggs (vols. i–ii, 1956, vols. iii–iv, 1959).
C.N.	*The Notebooks of Samuel Taylor Coleridge*, edited by K. Coburn (vol. i (two parts) 1957, vol. ii (two parts) 1962).
E.G.	*The Epic of Gilgamesh*, translated by N. K. Sandars (1960).
J.W.C.I.	*Journal of the Warburg and Courtauld Institutes.*
K.	*The Complete Writings of William Blake*, edited by Geoffrey Keynes (revised edition, 1957).
M.M.R.	M. P. Nilsson, *The Minoan–Mycenaean Religion and its Survival in Greek Religion* (revised edition, 1950).

PART ONE

THE PROBLEM

I

INTRODUCTORY

1

THIS book is about a particular form of the myth of paradise.[1] The most celebrated account of paradise, as we all know, occurs in Genesis, and is generally known as the story of the Fall. The Genesis story of man's expulsion from an ideal enclave combines much of the force of a great myth with a most tantalizing incoherence; and, as this is the form in which most of us first became acquainted with the idea of paradise, it is worth-while to remind ourselves at the outset of some of its notorious difficulties, although only the last of those that I shall mention bears directly upon our theme.

In the first place, the Genesis story ascribes an unaccountable offence to creatures of unsullied goodness, who are completely fulfilled and have no vacuity in their lives or cause for restlessness; and these supposedly once most fortunate of beings have been held responsible not only for a primal disaster but for every misery and imperfection of man. But why should we blame Eve for her offence, if it sprang inevitably from her character and situation? And how are we to understand it, if it did not?

Secondly, the concept of Evolution has led us to associate the emergence of any type of new complexity with a stage of experiment and error, and we have every reason to believe that all man's higher faculties, including moral consciousness, developed in this way. Man is a creature who not only makes mistakes but needs to make

[1] The word 'paradise' derives from the Old Persian *pairidaéza* (*pairi* = around +*diz* = to mould, to form), meaning an enclosed park or orchard. It is used in this book to refer to all related kinds of ideal enclave.

them, for that is how he grows and progresses. How then was Eve's mistake a culpable one?

Thirdly, why was there an authorized *agent provocateur* in the Garden to lure the species into degradation? Satan's retort in *Paradise Lost*, 'let him surer barr His Iron Gates', has more the impressiveness of the unimpeachably obvious than of heroic defiance, and no critic has yet squared it with Christian apologetics.

Fourthly, and most important for our purposes, the idea of life in a paradisial garden, whether sacred or profane, an endless prospect of harmony and repose, strikes us as a most oppressive one, unless we think of this existence as representing a short fleeting phase of equilibrium. Why did the Creator require Adam and Eve to remain immured in such a confine indefinitely?

I do not in fact believe that all these difficulties can be met, certainly not in terms of the doctrine of the Fall,[1] without falling back upon unconvincing sophistries, but on any view they must greatly add to the significance and interest of whatever alternative conceptions of the ideal enclave there may be. And if, because we find we cannot accept the passivity of its implicit ideal of harmony and repose, our attitude to the paradise of Genesis is on the whole one of thankfulness that, as Lionel Trilling puts it, 'by means of sin and the fall we managed to get ourselves expelled from that place', it will matter a great deal to us whether or not a satisfactory counter-ideal has ever found expression in myth.

My purpose is to establish that there is indeed such an alternative paradisial myth, and to trace certain persistent elements in its structure from Sumerian and Greek myth and visual imagery through selected themes in Renaissance literature and art, particularly the main plays of Shakespeare's final period, and thence by way of *Paradise Lost* to Coleridge. We shall begin by looking at a group of ancient works of literature and art which raise a perplexing and unavoidable problem as to how we should make sense of them, why they assumed the form they did, and what they signify. This group

---

[1] It is not within the scope of this book to evaluate the various hypotheses about the possible origin of the Genesis story, such as that advanced in T. Reik, *Myth and Guilt* (1956).

consists first of three important literary treatments of the ideal enclave in which the imaginative centre is provided by the configuration of tree and snake, and secondly of certain visualizations of the crucial latter motif alone. In the second part of the book I shall argue that these works of art in fact set forth, with the severe exactness of which only imaginative productions are capable, a reconciliation of two basic and permanent human ideals, which are opposed to one another. And I shall try to show that, as we realize more fully the nature of these elements within ourselves and consider other poetic and visual forms in which they have found no less precise expression, we come to see not only why the whole great tradition of earthly paradises and gardens of delight is unsatisfying but also what kind of ideal we need to put in its place.

II

The word 'myth' is used throughout this book to mean a story which, as well as corresponding with lasting patterns of thought and feeling as any narrative must that is to command attention, expresses them at a deep level with a definitive kind of economy and concentration. Where strongly mythopœic literature and art are concerned, any sort of dogmatic historicism is, I believe, misplaced and unprofitable. The essential point is very simply expressed by Blake, when he declares his belief in the perennial nature of the major themes and ideas which imagination presents to us:

> Visions of these eternal principles or characters of human life appear to poets, in all ages.[1]

Blake's interest in ancient wisdom, like that of the Italian Neoplatonists, was, of course, practical: it was to be used in the present. And so he considered that the archaic art and literature of all nations should be 'no less sacred than that of the Jews'.[2] But, in adopting his broad approach to early works of art, we shall only assume that some constituents of the human mind persist which can only be sufficiently expressed in symbolic form, and that the most subtle poetic structures which the mind creates at different times for this

---

[1] K. 571. [For abbreviations used in footnotes, see p. xi.]   [2] K. 578.

purpose tend not to become outdated. It follows that comparable new poetic forms are likely to bear important resemblances to old ones. And sometimes, of course, we must expect an early poetic form directly to influence a later one, because it is too definitively expressive to be forgotten or not to be used again after being rediscovered. If early mythopœic poetry has enduring relevance, it is plain that if we want to understand, say, a Sumerian myth, we ought to look to our present response, rather than wait upon what missing evidence about Sumerian ritual may yet emerge from the mounds of Nippur. This does not mean that we should underestimate the importance of the social conditions and institutions from which a particular myth originated. As Henri Frankfort has stressed,[1] the first civic communities were precarious structures needing the support of a mythical apparatus and their own presiding deity, and so the earliest myths, many of whose protagonists were gods and goddesses associated with particular cities, helped to justify the existing political order and maintain social cohesion. On the other hand, if we are persuaded of the fundamentally poetic character of myth, we shall be unable to accept as a wholesale explanation of all its manifestations the theory that myths are merely primitive attempts to explain social customs and biological facts; so that, for instance, the Genesis story must have been invented to explain the institution of patriarchy, why men labour in the fields, why women suffer pain in childbirth, and so forth. This view, it seems to me, arbitrarily belittles the intelligence of those who built the first civilizations and treats their imagination, with almost no justification at all, as having been inferior in range and subtlety to our own.

III

Whenever I refer to a myth or mythological figure and there is an early poetic source, I shall give the relevant part of it fully in translation; for only blind trust in knowledge by second-hand description would have us believe that the poetic form of a myth is unimportant, or that we can afford to depend upon a prosaic summary instead.

[1] *The Birth of Civilisation in the Near East* (1951), p. 51.

Myths are the most accurate means that the human mind has devised of representing its own immeasurably complex structure and content. They are essentially poetic formations, and express areas of thought and feeling where, as Blake puts it, 'ideas can only be given in their minutely appropriate words'. The basic correspondence between a great myth and the constitution of the mind is so strong that it can have many variations, and, provided they are truly poetic ones, it suffers no loss in this way. But summary deadens myth, and a single passage of mythopœic poetry or one great picture, sufficiently considered, will yield more than any number of references to myths or mythological figures. I shall also endeavour to rely as little as possible on general notions such as we so easily deceive ourselves that we know all about, because they are comfortingly familiar. Confronted by a great myth, an important mythopœic work of art, or a major symbol, we are inclined to ask, 'What does this represent?', meaning 'What general conception will do instead of this and let us out of the task of imaginative exploration and understanding?' We then come up with some well-tried abstraction (Fertility, Regeneration, Life, Order, the Unconscious) which may or may not vaguely embrace what the work of art presents with minute exactness, for on the whole we are much more disinclined to exert ourselves imaginatively than intellectually. But works of art cannot be reduced to concepts, and men do not bring forth radically imaginative productions to duplicate the work of abstract thought, or to express picturesquely what they could convey quite efficiently by general ideas. They create them because the intricacies of our mental life require a more subtle and sensitive medium of expression than abstract discourse can provide. And besides being inadequate and unenlightening in this field, abstractions tend to leave us cold. They ask nothing of us and do not touch our vital concerns. Thus it will be our aim to resist this ever-present temptation to try to cash poetic structures into imprecise and undemanding concepts, although some of these will be necessary to suggest an angle of approach and to give direction to our inquiry.

2

THEMES IN SUMERIAN AND
GREEK MYTH
AND VISUAL IMAGERY

WE begin, as we have said, by considering a group of early works of literature and art which are important in themselves and raise a problem of far-reaching consequence. Unfortunately, our knowledge of their historical origins is for the most part meagre and inconclusive. Indeed, if the main ideas presented later on had not forcibly led me back to where the ancient world shelves into the unascertainable, I should have preferred for this reason to set out from elsewhere.

I. GENESIS AND SUMERIAN MYTH

Before turning to the Sumerian poem which is the starting-point of our investigation, we must give some idea of its background.[1] One of the two most dramatic archaeological achievements of the last hundred years has been the discovery of the great Sumerian civilization which flourished in the delta of the Tigris and Euphrates during the third millennium B.C. As a result of this, we now know that the Sumerians, whose very name had until a little over a century ago vanished from the world, as well as being probably the first people to invent and develop an effective system of writing, created both an impressively powerful and sophisticated art and the earliest substantial literature that we possess. The Sumerian literary compositions, which contain a large and varied body of myth and epic telling of the deeds of gods and heroes, together with numerous hymns and lamentations, probably assumed more or less their

---

[1] For a fuller account see S. N. Kramer, *Sumerian Mythology* (revised edition, 1961).

known form in the second half of the third millennium B.C., and
they were inscribed on clay tablets by Sumerian scribes about
1750 B.C. Sumerian literature, as we know it, is at least a thousand
years older than Homer or Genesis. A great deal of this is now
available to us, thanks to the labours of Professor Kramer and other
scholars, although many tablets have still to be translated and new
ones are constantly being found. Some of the Sumerian stories we
know only through early Babylonian literature,[1] which is based on
the Sumerian and contains massive borrowings from it; for there
was all but complete continuity of culture between the Sumerians
and their Semitic conquerors, even when a new wave of nomadic
Amorites swept into Sumer from the Western Desert in the twen-
tieth century B.C. The Babylonians took over the religious ideas of
the Sumerians together with most of the Sumerian pantheon. They
also adopted the Sumerian hero-figures, including the most important and famous of them, Gilgamesh, the approximate Sumerian
equivalent of the Greek Heracles, whose adventures and quest
for immortality are recounted in *The Epic of Gilgamesh*.

Sumero-Babylonian literature shows striking correspondences
with some of the most important episodes and ideas in Genesis.
There are important similarities between the account of Creation
we are given in Genesis and the Sumero-Babylonian cosmogony, in
particular a common insistence that all things had a watery origin,
although in Sumero-Babylonian thought the great waters are from
before even the gods themselves. The Babylonian description of the
primordial element, an idea which will be of some importance for
us later on, runs:

> When on high the heaven had not been named,
> Firm ground below had not been called by name,
> Nought but primordial Apsu,[2] their begetter,
> (And) Mummu[3]-Tiamat,[4] she who bore them all,
> Their waters commingling as a single body;

---

[1] I use this expression as a convenient way of referring to literature contained in
texts, written in the Akkadian language, dating from the Old Babylonian Period
(2000–1600 B.C.).

[2] The fresh waters.   [3] Creatress.   [4] The marine waters, the sea.

No reed hut had been matted, no marsh land had appeared,
When no gods whatever had been brought into being,
Uncalled by name, their destinies undetermined—
Then it was that the gods were formed within them.[1]

Sumerian myth also has, like Genesis, its earthly paradise, the
'bright land of Dilmun', watered by the sun-god, where there is
abundance of grain, where there is neither sickness nor death, and
the wolf is at peace with the lamb.[2] And we find in Sumero-
Babylonian literature the celebrated sacred tree, prototype of the
Tree of Life in the Genesis story, whose care was the special responsibility of the king,[3] and which we see represented so often on
Babylonian seals, and the sanctuary in which it stands:

In Eridu[4] there is a black *kiskanu*-tree
    growing in a pure place,
its appearance is lapis-lazuli,
    erected on the *Apsū*.
Enki,[5] when walking there, filleth Eridu with abundance.
    In the foundation thereof is the place of the underworld,
in the resting-place is the chamber of Nammu.[6]
    In its holy temple there is a grove, casting its shadow,
therein no man goeth to enter.
    In the midst are the Sun-god and the Sovereign of heaven,
in between the river with the two mouths.[7]

But there is no story of temptation and expulsion.
    Ever since the discovery of Sumero-Babylonian literature biblical
scholars have ransacked it in vain for a possible source of the story

---

[1] *A.N.E.T.*, p. 60. I quote this account, although it is from the relatively late text
of the Babylonian *Creation Epic*, as vividly presenting the conception. The same idea
of primordial Ocean is found in a Sumerian text listing the names of the gods, where
the goddess Nammu, who represents primordial ocean, is described as the mother
who gave birth to heaven and earth. Kramer, op. cit., p. 39.
[2] It is described in the myth *Enki and Ninhursag*, *A.N.E.T.*, p. 37.
[3] See G. Widengren, *The King and the Tree of Life* (Uppsala, 1951).
[4] A city in southern Mesopotamia, one of the earliest cult-centres, the modern
Abu Shahrein.
[5] The water-god, patron of the city of Eridu.
[6] See footnote 1 above.   [7] Widengren, op. cit., pp. 5–6.

of the Fall.[1] Not only have they so far failed to find one, but there is a strong reason why it is unlikely that any such Sumerian story will ever come to light, and it has a special interest for us, because it shows more clearly than anything else the kind of religious outlook underlying the Sumerian poem we are about to look at and how different it is from the one we find in Genesis. This reason becomes apparent if we consider the theme in whose treatment the strongest correspondences between Genesis and Sumero-Babylonian literature are to be found, the story of the Flood. In the Sumerian and Babylonian Flood-stories, the gods decide to send the deluge simply because mankind is becoming too numerous and too noisy:

> The land became wide, the people became numerous,
> The land bellowed like wild oxen.
> The god was disturbed by their uproar.
> Enlil[2] heard their clamour
> And said to the great gods:
> 'Oppressive has become the clamor of mankind.
> By their uproar they prevent sleep.'[3]

Man's ceaseless clamour disturbs and annoys the gods. And so at Enlil's instigation they decide in assembly to destroy both him and his cult-centres, only to shrink in terror at the sight of the deluge which they themselves have sent and to reproach themselves bitterly, when they see the havoc that they have brought about:

> Even the gods were terrified at the flood, they fled to the highest
> heaven, the firmament of Anu;[4] they crouched against the walls,

[1] The only serious attempt to meet this requirement is the fascinating and ingenious deployment of serpentine motifs in Sumerian and Babylonian art and artefacts in P. Toscanne's study *Études sur le Serpent*, 'Mémoires de la délégation en Perse', Series IV, vol. 12 (Paris 1911). Toscanne is ready to detect a seductive intent from the very juxtaposition of serpent with tree or man-like figure (as in the famous Smith Cylinder in the British Museum). His case would be thin in any eventwithout corroboration from any importaut literary material. But he does not attempt to substantiate his interpretation of the forms against other plausible explanations, and the intriguing figures in his essay need to be scanned with some appreciation of the variety of other animals that appear on Sumerian and Babylonian artefacts juxtaposed to trees, men, and gods. See, for instance, N. Perrot, *Les représentations de l'arbre sacré sur les monuments de Mésopotamie et d'Élam* (Paris, 1937).

[2] God of the winds and the earth, lord of the city of Nippur.

[3] From the Atrahasis fragment, *A.N.E.T.*, p. 104.

[4] Father of gods and god of the firmament, supreme god of the Sumero-Babylonian pantheon.

cowering like curs. Then Ishtar[1] the sweet-voiced Queen of Heaven cried out like a woman in travail: 'Alas the days of old are turned to dust because I commanded evil; why did I command this evil in the council of all the gods? I commanded wars to destroy the people, but are they not my people, for I brought them forth? Now like the spawn of fish they float in the ocean.' The great gods of heaven and hell wept, they covered their mouths.[2]

What mainly distinguishes the Genesis story of the Flood from the Sumerian and Babylonian accounts is Yahweh's fearful denunciation of human sinfulness:

> And God saw that the wickedness of man was great in the earth, and that every imagination of the thoughts of his heart was only evil continually. And it repented the Lord that he had made man on the earth, and it grieved him at his heart. And the Lord said, I will destroy man whom I have created from the face of the earth; both man, and beast, and the creeping thing, and the fowls of the air; for it repenteth me that I have made them.[3]

Whereas in the Sumero-Babylonian story the Flood is the result of irrational and destructive anger on the part of the gods, in Genesis the deluge is sent as a judgement upon man for his wickedness. When mankind has been destroyed, apart from the one favoured survivor and his family, Yahweh promises never to send a second flood, but he does not in any way reproach himself for what he has done. Indeed he stresses yet again the inherent wickedness of man, declaring that 'the imagination of man's heart is evil from his youth'.[4] The overwhelming impression is that a transition has been made, very broadly comparable to the movement from a 'shame-culture' to a 'guilt-culture'[5] which we see reflected in the development of Greek literature after the age of Homer: the progression into the sombre world of Sophocles and Aeschylus, where at every step man's life is overshadowed by fear of offending the ever-watchful gods, leaving behind the religious and mental climate of Homer's

---

[1] The Sumerian Inanna; goddess of love, fertility, and war.
[2] *E.G.*, p. 107.
[3] Genesis 6: 5–7.
[4] Genesis 8: 21.
[5] See E. R. Dodds, *The Greeks and the Irrational* (1951), Ch. ii.

world, which had allowed man to stand in considerable boldness before his divine superiors, so that it was possible for Helen to ask of the disguised Aphrodite herself, 'Lady of mysteries, what is the object of this mummery?',[1] and for Diomedes to shout at the goddess, 'Daughter of Zeus, be off from this battle and leave war alone. Is it not enough for you to set your traps for feeble women-folk?'[2] This transition from a conception of the gods as vengeful and dangerous to belief in a deity, or several, whose anger is denunciatory and retributive is a great watershed in the history of Western thought, and one which we are as yet far from fully understanding. It is absolutely plain, however, that the Sumero-Babylonian Flood-narratives lie on one side of it, and that the Genesis account is on the other.

The same contrast strikes us if we consider such slender Sumero-Babylonian parallels to the story of the Fall as there are. In *The Epic of Gilgamesh* the hero, as he travels home with Urshanabi the ferry-man, bearing the youth-restoring flower, whose whereabouts has been revealed to him by the semi-divine hero Utnapishtim, has it snatched from him by a snake while he is bathing:

Gilgamesh saw a well of cool water and he went down and bathed; but deep in the pool there was lying a serpent, and the serpent sensed the sweetness of the flower. It rose out of the water and snatched it away, and immediately it sloughed its skin and returned to the well. Then Gilgamesh sat down and wept, the tears ran down his face, and he took the hand of Urshanabi: 'O Urshanabi, was it for this that I toiled with my hands, is it for this I have wrung out my heart's blood? For myself I have gained nothing; not I, but the beast of the earth has joy of it now. Already the stream has carried it twenty leagues back to the channels where I found it. I found a sign and now I have lost it. Let us leave the boat on the bank and go.'[3]

And in this way Gilgamesh learns at last that the will of the gods is implacably opposed to man's quest for immortality. The early Babylonian myth *Adapa*[4] tells a rather similar story. Adapa, the hero,

---

[1] *Iliad*, iii. 399.   [2] *Iliad*, v. 348.
[3] *E.G.*, p. 114.   [4] *A.N.E.T.*, p. 101.

is summoned before Anu, the God of Heaven, because by uttering a curse he has broken one of the wings of the South Wind. Anu is munificently clement and offers him the food and water of *life*, but Adapa, who has been forewarned by his father that he will be offered the food and water of *death*, refuses and receives his dismissal:

> Thou wilt not live. . . . Take him and bring him back to his earth.

In both these stories, immortality is placed within man's grasp only to be snatched from him at the last moment. Both of them express the same concern that the Genesis story shows with the problem of why men have to die. But they entirely lack the tempter, the temptation, the great offence, and the whole context of well-earned condemnation that give urgency and drama to the story of the Fall. It is merely the divine jealousy which requires that man shall not live for ever. 'When the gods created man', Gilgamesh is told, 'they allotted to him death but life they retained in their own keeping.'[1] Once more it is clear that the Sumero-Babylonian stories are on one side of the divide between 'shame-culture' and 'guilt-culture', and that the Genesis story is on the opposite one:

> And unto Adam he said, Because thou hast hearkened unto the voice of thy wife, and hast eaten of the tree, of which I commanded thee, saying, 'Thou shalt not eat of it'; cursed is the ground for thy sake; in sorrow shalt thou eat of it all the days of thy life; thorns also and thistles shall it bring forth to thee; and thou shalt eat the herb of the field; in the sweat of thy face shalt thou eat bread, till thou return unto the ground; for out of it wast thou taken; for dust thou art, and unto dust shalt thou return.[2]

Before a god such as this man's proper place is in the dust of self-abasement. The Sumero-Babylonian gods and goddesses, on the other hand, are fundamentally uncensorious. They withhold immortality from man, not as retribution for his sin but because, like the gods of Homer, they are determined to keep the best things for themselves, just as they send the Flood, not in order to denounce man's wickedness but because their human underlings are multiplying too fast and are becoming a nuisance to them. Divided in

---

[1] *E.G.*, p. 99.   [2] Genesis 3: 17–19.

council, capriciously benign or malevolent, they have no wish and no right to issue the kind of denunciation *de haut en bas* which is so essential a part of the story of the Fall. And so, if Sumerian mythology includes a profound and searching treatment of the paradisial idea, it is certain to be radically different from the Genesis story and to mirror quite another mental world.

II. TREE AND SNAKE IN SUMERIAN AND GREEK MYTH

Now let us look at a Sumerian myth which has received little attention, although much of it has been available in translation since 1938.[1] It is the story of the Huluppu-Tree which Inanna, goddess of love, fertility, and war, better known under her Babylonian name of Ishtar, found on the bank of the Euphrates and planted in her sacred garden. After an introductory passage setting the main action at a time shortly after the Creation and the assumption by the gods of their various spheres of influence, it continues:

On that day a tree, a huluppu-tree, a tree—
On the bank of the pure Euphrates it had been planted;
The Euphrates was its drinking water—
Mightily the South Wind plucked at its base, tore at its crown;
The Euphrates on its waters carried it off.
A lady walking in fear at the word of Anu,
Walking in fear at the word of Enlil,
Seized the tree in her hand and brought it to Uruk;
'To pure Inanna's holy garden thou shalt bring it.'
The lady tended the tree with her hand, she let it stand at her foot
The lady tended the tree with her hand, she let it stand at her foot.
'When at last shall I have a holy throne that I may sit on it?' concerning it she said;
'When at last shall I have a holy bed that I may lie on it?' concerning it she said.
The tree grew large, but she could not cut off its bark.
At its base the snake who knows no charm had set up for itself a nest,
In its crown the Zu-bird[2] had placed his young,

---

[1] Kramer, *Gilgamesh and the Huluppu-Tree*. Oriental Institute of the University of Chicago, Assyriological Studies (Chicago, 1931–   ), No. 10. Kramer gives a full account of the second part in *Sumerian Mythology*.   [2] A thieving bird.

In its midst Lilith[1] had built for herself a house.
The ever shouting maid, the rejoicer of all hearts,
The pure Inanna, how she weeps!
At the break of day, as the horizon became light,
The lady Inanna
To Gilgamesh speaks.

[There follows a repetitive section of 38 lines.]

In the matter concerning which his sister had spoken to him,
In that matter her brother, the hero Gilgamesh, stood by her.
Armor weighing as much as fifty minas he fastened at his waist—
That which weighed as much as fifty minas he treated like thirty
    shekels.
His bronze ax, his ax of the road,
His ax of seven talents and seven minas, he seized in his hand.
At its base he smote the snake who knows no charm;
In its crown the Zu-bird took its young
And brought it to the mountain;
In its midst Lilith destroyed her house
And escaped to the desert places.
The tree, he plucked at its base, he tore at its crown;
The sons of his city who had accompanied him cut down its crown.
Unto the pure Inanna for her throne he gives it.
For her bed he gives it.
He, its base into his pukku he makes,
Its crown into his mikku[2] he makes.

In the second part of the story comes disaster. The parts of the
tree which Gilgamesh has appropriated, presumably as a reward for
killing the snake, suddenly fall into the Underworld 'because of the
crying of the maidens'. Much distressed at being unable to recover
them, Gilgamesh sends down his servant and companion Enkidu
with an elaborate warning about taboos he should observe 'lest the
dead heroes will come forth like enemies'. But Enkidu neglects these
instructions and the Underworld seizes him. So finally the water-
god Enki, god of wisdom, sends the sun-god Utu on a successful
mission to retrieve Enkidu. The poem ends with the interrogation

[1] A demoness.
[2] The 'pukku' and 'mikku' are probably a drum and a drum-stick.

of Enkidu about the treatment accorded in the Underworld to various persons he has seen.

The Sumerian myth *Gilgamesh and the Huluppu-Tree* is much more complex than any surviving version of its Greek parallel, the myth of Heracles and the Apples of the Hesperides, in which Heracles is sent by Eurystheus to the Hesperidean garden to fetch the golden apples which Earth brought forth as her wedding gift to Zeus and Hera, compels the Old Man of the Sea to show him the way, and either kills the serpent guarding the apples[1] or holds up the sky while Atlas plucks them for him.[2] The double role of Inanna, at once gardener and materialist, the three tiers of denizens, the obscure regression of the magical objects into the Underworld, and the quest to recover them have no equivalent in the Greek story and call for separate discussion. My present concern, however, is with the imaginative centre of the Sumerian story, with the tree and the snake at its base which obstructs Inanna's scheme for making furniture out of it, and here the correspondence with the Hesperides myth is very close. The Hesperides myth likewise has as its central image a serpent-guarded tree, although unfortunately there remains no early poetic presentation of this or of the story as a whole. There are fragmentary references to the tree and its guardian in Hesiod:

> Next she [Night] gave birth to Blame and painful Grief, and the Hesperian nymphs who guard the beautiful golden apples and the trees which bear that fruit on the further shore of great Ocean. . . .[3]

> The youngest of all the children that Ceto conceived from her union with Phorcys was the fierce Dragon which in dark underground depths guards the golden apples with his huge coils.[4]

For Euripides the Garden of the Hesperides is an inaccessible divine precinct, barred to man, at the edge of the sea:

> And O for that quiet garden by the Western sea
> Where the daughters of Evening sing
> Under the golden apple-tree;

---

[1] Euripides, *Hercules Furens*, 394 ff. Apollonius Rhodius, *Argonautica*, iv. 1396 ff.
[2] Pherekydes ap. schol. Apoll. Rhod. iv. 1396. Apollodorus, II. v. 11.
[3] *Theogony*, 213 ff.   [4] *Theogony*, 333–5.

> Where the bold sailor wandering
> Finds the Ocean-god has barred
> His Westward path over the purple waste![1]

The second-century Greek mythographer Apollodorus gives a variant of the tale in some detail but is pedestrian.[2] The most poetic treatment of any length is that of Ovid, who situates this domain of Atlas at the world's extreme verge:

> Here, far surpassing all men in huge bulk of body, was Atlas, of the stock of Iapetus. He ruled this edge of the world and the sea which spread its waters to receive the Sun's panting horses and his weary car. A thousand flocks he had, and as many herds, wandering at will over the grassy plains; and no other realm was near to hem in his land. A tree he had whose leaves were of gleaming gold, concealing golden branches and golden fruits. 'Good sir', said Perseus, addressing him, 'if glory of high birth means anything to you, Jove is my father; or if you admire great deeds, you surely will admire mine. I crave your hospitality and a chance to rest.' But Atlas bethought him of an old oracle, which Themis of Parnassus had given: 'Atlas, the time will come when your tree will be spoiled of its gold, and he who gets the glory of this spoil will be Jove's son.' Fearing this, Atlas had enclosed his orchard with massive walls and had put a huge dragon there to watch it; and he kept off all strangers from his boundaries.[3]

But for a truly sharp impression of the snake-encircled tree and its ambience of intense mystery we have to look to such visual treatments as that on the lower frieze of the vase-painting by the late fifth-century Meidias painter (Pl. 1), where we see Heracles resting in the garden of the Hesperides and one of the Hesperidean nymphs

---

[1] *Hippolytus*, 742-5.

[2] 'When the labours had been performed in eight years and a month, Eurystheus ordered Hercules, as an eleventh labour, to fetch golden apples from the Hesperides, for he did not acknowledge the labour of the cattle of Augeas nor that of the hydra. These apples were not, as some have said, in Libya, but on Atlas among the Hyperboreans. They were presented by Earth to Zeus after his marriage with Hera, and guarded by an immortal dragon with a hundred heads, offspring of Typhon and Echidna, which spoke with many and divers sorts of voices. With it the Hesperides also were on guard, to wit, Aegle, Erythia, Hesperia, and Arethusa.' *Library*, II. v. 11. It will be noted that Apollodorus plants the garden among the legendary Hyperboreans, who were usually thought of as being inhabitants of the far North.

[3] *Metamorphoses* iv. 631-48.

Plate 1. Athenian Hydria, *c.* 410 B.C., by the Meidias Painter. On the lower frieze, Heracles resting in the garden of the Hesperides (*British Museum*)

reaching towards the golden apples. The garden is represented on numerous vase-paintings, but this is almost certainly the finest visualization we have. It manifests the compelling power of the myth and at once enables us to understand why its influence survived.

At this point we also need to have before us in concrete form the other important snake-protected tree in Greek mythology, the one on which hangs the Golden Fleece in Apollonius of Rhodes' fourth-century account of the Voyage of the Argonauts, although this Greek saga has some of the diffuseness that we associate with *Märchen* as opposed to great myth. It is a tale of great antiquity, and even in Homer Jason's vessel is referred to as 'the celebrated Argo'.[1] At the point in the story which concerns us, the Argonauts have arrived at Colchis. Protected by Medea's magic ointment, Jason has performed the task set him by King Aeetes, has ploughed the great field, sowed the serpent's teeth in the ground, and slain the armed men that spring up from the seed. Medea has fled from her father's palace to the ship Argo under cover of night, and has promised Jason that she will put the guardian snake to sleep. And now, just before dawn, the Argonauts row Jason and Medea with all speed to a point near the sacred wood where stands the great serpent-guarded oak:

Here, then, under Argus' direction, the crew set the pair ashore. A path led them to the sacred wood, where they were making for the huge oak on which the fleece was hung, bright as a cloud reddened by the fiery beams of the rising sun. But the serpent with his sharp unsleeping eyes had seen them coming and now confronted them, stretching out his long neck and hissing fearfully. The high banks of the river and the deep recesses of the wood threw back the sound, and far away from Titanian Aea it reached the ears of Colchians living by the outfall of Lycus, the river that parts from the loud waters of Araxes to unite his sacred stream with that of Phasis and flow in company with him till both debouch into the Caucasian Sea. Babies sleeping in their mothers' arms were startled by the hiss, and their anxious mothers waking in alarm hugged them closer to their breasts.

---

[1] *Odyssey*, xii. 70.

The monster in his sheath of horny scales rolled forward his interminable coils, like the eddies of black smoke that spring from smouldering logs and chase each other from below in endless convolutions. But as he writhed he saw the maiden take her stand, and heard her in her sweet voice invoking Sleep, the conqueror of the gods, to charm him. She also called on the night-wandering Queen of the world below to countenance her efforts. Jason from behind looked on in terror. But the giant snake, enchanted by her song, was soon relaxing the whole length of his serrated spine and smoothing out his multitudinous undulations, like a dark and silent swell rolling across a sluggish sea. Yet his grim head still hovered over them and the cruel jaws threatened to snap them up. But Medea, chanting a spell, dipped a fresh sprig of juniper in her brew and sprinkled his eyes with her most potent drug; and as the all-pervading magic scent spread round his head, sleep fell on him. Stirring no more, he let his jaw sink to the ground, and his innumerable coils lay stretched out far behind, spanning the deep wood. Medea called to Jason and he snatched the golden fleece from the oak. But she herself stayed where she was, smearing the wild one's head with a magic salve, till Jason urged her to come back to the ship and she left the sombre grove of Ares.[1]

Ovid's description of the episode is much shorter and considerably more poetic:

There remained the task of putting to sleep the ever-watchful serpent with magic herbs. Distinguished by a crest, a three-forked tongue and curving fangs, it was the awful guardian of the golden tree. When Jason had sprinkled upon him the Lethaean juice of a certain herb and had recited three times the words that bring peaceful slumber, which still the raging sea and swift-flowing rivers, sleep came to those eyes which had never known sleep before, and the heroic son of Aeson gained the golden fleece.[2]

In Ovid's version of the story, Jason bears away the sleeping snake as well as the fleece, and the Argonauts carry it back with them to Iolchos.

All three myths point to one question as being crucial and inescapable: what is signified by the snake-encircled tree? Why

---

[1] *Argonautica*, iv. 121–66.   [2] *Metamorphoses*, vii. 149–56.

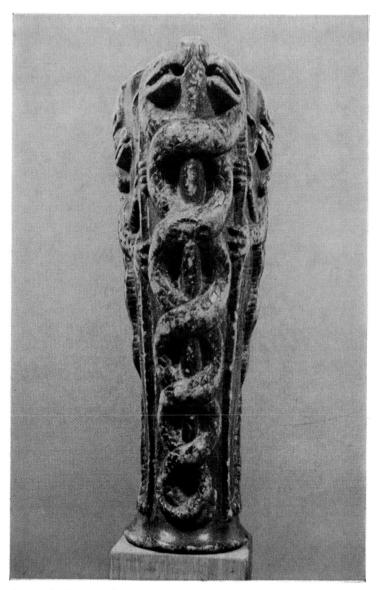

Plate 2. Libation vase of Gudea, *c.* 2150 B.C., showing caduceus, flanked by two supporting dragons (*Paris, Louvre*)

does it occupy a central position in the structure of each of them, exercising a mysterious appeal to which we still respond and which, as we shall see later in this book, deeply influenced at least one and almost certainly two of our own greatest poets? No one is likely to suppose that these three stories came to have the same imaginative centre by accident, or that anything less than some stringent necessity can account for this correspondence. We now turn to two visual images, one Sumerian and the other Greek, which raise in a slightly different form the same fundamental and clamant problem.

III. TREE AND SNAKE IN SUMERIAN AND GREEK VISUAL IMAGERY

Carved on the magnificent green steatite Libation Vase of Gudea (Pl. 2) stands a powerful and enigmatic snake-encircled pole or caduceus, flanked by two supporting dragons. Snake-adorned poles and staffs combine the same elements as the snake-encircled tree on a smaller scale. And the tree–branch–sceptre nexus in the Old Testament, the Christian legend that Moses' rod was a branch cut by Adam from one of the two forbidden trees in paradise, the devotional tradition which treats the Cross as the one and only precious tree, the substitution of the may-pole for the may-tree in European folk-ritual, and many like examples, show how vitally important for an image of this kind is the link between part and original whole. Such emblems can embody in miniature mythopœic ideas similar to those set forth by their larger counterparts, although they may also degenerate into empty, or almost empty, conventional signs.

Gudea, ruler of the Sumerian city of Lagash in the twenty-second century B.C., patronized the arts on a scale unequalled even in that remarkable period. He rebuilt not less than fifteen temples in Lagash, and commissioned a whole series of imposing portrait-sculptures, representing himself at different ages, more than thirty examples of which survive, the finest collection being now in the Louvre. His vase bears the inscription 'To the god Ningizzida, his god, Gudea, *ensi* of Lagash, for the Prolongation of his life has dedicated (this).' It is generally believed that the caduceus represents the god himself, and beyond doubt it is at least very closely associated with him. Frankfort comments:

There is no doubt that the entwined serpents represent here the god, the dragons appearing in the entirely subservient position of attendants, or more precisely of guardians at the gate of the sanctuary, which is rendered in abbreviation by two archaic doorposts, just as the god himself is only indicated by the caduceus.[1]

Ningizzida,[2] 'Lord of the true Tree', emerges from obscure origins into a short phase of eminence as Gudea's special tutelary god. Gudea refers to him as 'my god' elsewhere, and another inscription runs 'he takes me by the hand and leads me into the presence of (name of god)'. The stele of Gudea in the Berlin Museum and the seal of Gudea graphically represent Ningizzida in this role. On the Berlin stele (Pl. 3*a*) Ningizzida, from whose shoulders issue two serpents, leads Gudea forward, holding him by the wrist, into the presence of a deity, whose figure is unfortunately missing from the relief. And on the seal of Gudea (Pl. 3*b*) we see Ningizzida, once more with two serpents issuing from his shoulders, leading Gudea towards the seated figure of Enki, god of water and of wisdom. After the lifetime of Gudea, Ningizzida's development, although still connected with the Underworld, becomes obscure. In relation to Gudea, however, and at the time when he was represented by the caduceus, his role was plainly that of mediator between man and a higher level of divinity.[3]

The nearest Greek counterpart of the Sumerian caduceus is, of course, the famous snake-staff of Hermes,[4] which we see in countless representations of him and which we should probably know best

---

[1] 'Gods and Myths on Sargonid Seals', *Iraq*, vol. i (1934).

[2] For further discussion of Ningizzida see A. L. Frothingham, 'Babylonian Origin of Hermes the snake-god and of the caduceus', *American Journal of Archaeology*, vol. xx (1916), and E. D. van Buren, 'The God Ningizzida', *Iraq*, vol. i (1934). He was sufficiently important for Ur (dingir) Ningizzida, 'servant of the god Ningizzida', to have been a common name in all classes of society throughout the Third Dynasty of Ur.

[3] If, as is believed, he is to be identified with Gizzida, joint keeper with Tammuz of Anu's gate in the myth *Adapa*, this would be a congruous office.

[4] I pass over the snake-staff of Asklepios because both in Greek culture and in the European tradition he is a minor figure as compared with Hermes.

Plate 3a. Stele of Gudea,
c. 2150 B.C. Ningizzida leads
Gudea into the presence of a
deity (p. 22) (*Berlin, Vorderasiatisches Museum*)

Plate 3b. Seal of
Gudea. Ningizzida
leads Gudea to-
wards Enki, god of
water and of wis-
dom (p. 22)

through Botticelli's realization of him in *Primavera* (Pl. 5*a*), if the staff were visible in most reproductions. It has been convincingly argued against a Babylonian origin of Hermes' staff that its top was originally formed of interlaced twigs, and that it developed from a snakeless half-closed figure of eight.[1] However, when classical research arrives at the stage of marshalling careful arguments of this kind against the transmission of an emblem, we may provisionally expect at least an underlying resemblance.

Hermes in his developed form is known to us as a mediator, the divine messenger and guide of souls to the Underworld. He is believed originally to have been a pastoral deity, a god of flocks, or possibly a god of wayfarers, and he was also closely associated with boundaries and boundary-stones, but he came to acquire not only the especially important roles we have just mentioned but a variety of other ones as well, god of eloquence, patron of music, and leader of the Graces and the Nymphs. We need not depend, however, upon a mythographer's prosaic summary of his attributes, because there is a major early poetic treatment of these at the beginning of the Homeric *Hymn to Hermes*, which is devoted to his celebrated exploits on his first day alive:

Muse, sing of Hermes, Zeus and Maia's son, lord of Cyllene and Arcadia, rich in flocks, luck-bringing messenger of the immortals, issue of the love between Zeus and Maia, that nymph with lovely hair—a shy goddess avoiding the company of the immortal gods and living in a deep shady cave. There the son of Cronos would lie with her, unseen by deathless gods and mortal men, after sweet sleep had overcome white-armed Hera. And, when great Zeus's purpose was fulfilled and the tenth moon was come, she was delivered of her son, and a marvel happened: she bore a son of many stratagems, smoothly cunning, a robber, a cattle driver, a bringer of dreams, a watcher by night, a thief at the gates, who soon performed wonderful deeds among the immortal gods. Born at break of day, at noon he played on the lyre, and in the evening he stole the cattle of far-shooting Apollo— on the fourth day of the month, for that was the day queenly Maia gave birth to him.[2]

[1] J. W. M. De Waele, *The Magic Staff or Rod in Graeco-Italian Antiquity* (1927), pp. 42 ff.   [2] *Homeric Hymn to Hermes*, 1–19.

Throughout Homer the role of Hermes in relation to men is that of guide and deliverer, and he is represented as being of all the gods the most friendly to man. When Zeus assigns to him the task of escorting the aged Priam on his dangerous journey to and from the tent of Achilles, he prefaces his command with the words, 'Hermes, you love above all others to companion a man.'[1] Homer's most poetic description of Hermes comes when he is sent to rescue Ulysses from the sleep in which the nymph Calypso has knit up his senses:

> Zeus had spoken. His messenger, the Giant-killer, obeyed at once and bound under his feet the lovely sandals of untarnishable gold that carried him with the speed of the wind over the water or the boundless earth; and he picked up the wand which he can use at will to cast a sleep upon our eyes or wake us from the soundest sleep. With this wand in his hand, the mighty Giant-slayer made his flight. From the upper air he dropped to the Pierian range, and from there swooped down on the sea, and skimmed the waves like a sea-mew drenching the feathers of its wings with spray as it pursues the fish down desolate gulfs of the unharvested deep. So Hermes rode the unending waves, till at length he reached the remote island of Ogygia, where he stepped on to the shore from the blue waters of the sea. . . .[2]

The finest realization in Homer of Hermes' function as guide of souls to the Underworld occurs at the end of the *Odyssey*, when he accompanies the spirits of the dead suitors during their passage to Hades:

> Meanwhile Cyllenian Hermes was gathering in the souls of the Suitors, armed with the splendid golden wand that he can use at will to cast a spell on our eyes or wake us from the soundest sleep. He roused them up and marshalled them with this, and they obeyed his summons gibbering like bats that squeak and flutter in the depths of some mysterious cave when one of them has fallen from the rocky roof, losing his hold on his clustered friends. With such shrill discord the company set out in Hermes' charge, following the Deliverer down the dark paths of decay. Past Ocean Stream, past the White Rock,

---

[1] *Iliad*, xxiv. 334.   [2] *Odyssey*, v. 43–57.

past the Gates of the Sun and the region of dreams they went, and before long they reached the meadow of asphodel, which is the dwelling-place of souls, the disembodied wraiths of men.[1]

I do not want to suggest for a moment that the Sumerian Ningizzida was historically the prototype of Hermes,[2] but on the other hand it would be perverse to ignore the similarity between both the role and the emblem assigned to Hermes and those associated with that earlier representative go-between. As we are not attempting a reconstruction of ancient religion, the all but impossible problem of assigning even rough positions on the obscure historical lattice-work of cult and belief does not arise. Nevertheless, Sumerians and Greeks shared not only parallel myths of which the serpent-guarded tree in its divine precinct was the central feature but also visual images combining in miniature the same elements as does this configuration, and associated with comparable gods. What is the reason for these correspondences? And why did both peoples assign specifically to a figure who mediates between gods and men an image which unites on a smaller scale the same constituents as the one they made the imaginative centre of the ideal enclave? The answer to these questions plainly turns upon the crucial significance of the snake-encircled tree, and we cannot expect to find it so long as the meaning of this image continues to elude us.

IV. TREE AND SNAKE ON GREEK HERO-RELIEFS

At this stage of our inquiry, we cannot afford to overlook the unforgettable representations of the snake-encircled tree which appear on Greek hero-reliefs in the Late Classical and Hellenistic periods. But first we must say something about the reliefs themselves. Throughout historic times the proper burial of the dead was of the very greatest concern to the Greeks, as we can see from the elaborate funerals in Homer and the importance of refusal to perform or allow this pious office as a leading theme in Greek

---

[1] *Odyssey*, xxiv. 1–14.
[2] For the case in favour of the Minoan origin of Hermes see J. Chittenden, 'The Master of Animals', *Hesperia*, 1947.

tragedy; and in Greek religious practice as a whole one of the
most important elements was the making of offerings, regularly
and upon special occasions, at the tombs of the dead. These were
apparently thought of, at least from the time of Homer onwards,
in an unsystematic but typically human way, as being shadowy
inhabitants of distant Hades, yet at the same time as being united
with the powers of the Underworld and also, reflecting another
stratum of belief, formidably present for good or ill in the region
of their graves. From the early sixth century, when human
figures first appear regularly on Greek gravestones and commemorative monuments, reliefs of this kind fall into two main
groups. On the one hand there are what have every appearance
of being commemorative representations, highly idealized, but no
more so, superficially at least, than such memorials generally are;
and with the contentious problems raised by these transparently
clear yet elusive sculptures we need not here concern ourselves.[1]
In the other main group, consisting of the so called hero-reliefs, the
idealization is far greater than pious memory would require or
explain. A partially deified main figure first becomes a strikingly
recognizable type about the middle of the sixth century on the
imposing Spartan ancestor-reliefs, where typically we see two
august and hieratic figures seated side by side, ancestor and
ancestress, and a little group of diminutive worshippers, representing their descendants, who approach with offerings suitable for the
dead, a cock, a flower, a pomegranate. These figures were once
supposed to represent gods and goddesses of the Underworld, Hades
and his queen Persephone, but they are now generally thought to
be ancestor-figures, reflecting the strong Spartan cult of ancestors,
once living men and women who have become united and identified

[1] Such evidence as we have confirms the immediate, often poignant, impression
which most of these reliefs give of being visualizations of those who have died. (See
K. Fr. Johansen, *The Attic Grave-Reliefs of the Classical Period* (1951), pp. 148 ff.) It was
of these reliefs that Rilke wrote:
Are you not amazed to see on the Attic Grave-stones the circumspection
Of the human gesture? Were not love and farewell
So gently laid on their shoulders, as if they were of another
Substance than with us?
Duino Elegies I.

Plate 4. The snake-encircled tree:

a. Fourth-century Thyrean relief
(*Athens, National Museum*)

b. Hellenistic relief from Pergamon
(*Istanbul, Archaeological Museum*)

Plate 4. The snake-encircled tree:

c. Fourth-century relief from Piraeus
(*Athens, National Museum*)

d. Hellenistic relief from Samos
(*Samos Museum*)

with the powers of the Underworld, thus taking on much of the status of gods. One very common feature of these reliefs is a snake, looking over the ancestor-figure's chair or drinking from his wine-cup, and we cannot be at all sure whether this represents the soul of the dead man, as was believed at one time, his Underworld familiar, or some part of the complex of chthonian powers with which he has become associated. Also frequently included—and in a moment we shall be looking at later examples of these animal figures—are a horse and a dog. It has been suggested that these may have a mythological reference, the horse being connected with Hades and his chariot and the dog with Hecate and her hell-hounds or with the dog-headed monster Cerberus,[1] but this view has not won wide support and it seems more probable that the horse and dog are the dead man's earthly companions, who once proclaimed his knightly rank, and that the same feelings that brought about their ennobling role in this life carried them over into the next.

In broad line of descent from these Spartan reliefs, at any rate in conception, are the heroizing reliefs of the early fourth and later centuries, on which the partially deified principal figure generally reclines at a banquet or is shown as a horseman, together with his horse. Once again we often meet the little procession of worshippers who come to do homage, or it may be a single worshipper, and also the horse and the dog that appear on the Spartan reliefs. Another regular feature of the hero-reliefs is a female figure equal in stature to the hero, recalling the Spartan consort-ancestress, who stands beside him and pours him a cup of wine. These sculptures are an expression of the immensely popular and widespread cult of heroes, although it is often impossible to say whether the central figure represents one from among the vast throng of established heroes, national and local, mythical and historical, held in reverence by the Greeks, or whether he is an ordinary dead man who has just been raised to heroic status, for the band of acknowledged heroes was increasingly enlarged by fresh recruits from among the recently dead. The Greeks venerated a great number of hero-figures of various grades and kinds, feeling them no doubt to be nearer and

[1] Furtwängler, *Ath. Mitt.* vii. 163.

more approachable than the gods, and hero tombs and shrines were scattered all over Greece. Sometimes the name of the hero is recorded, if it is mythologically or otherwise important, but more often there is only some such anonymous legend as 'to the Leader' or 'to the Lord Hero', and very commonly there is no inscription at all. Heroes resembled ancestors, from whose cult they are thought to have developed, in that they were once mortal men and still exercised power from beyond the grave, but unlike the ordinary dead they were regarded as important enough to be honoured by a circle of devotees wider, often wider by far, than the family to which they belonged. They were, so to speak, public ancestor-figures, required to perform on a larger scale the traditional ancestral role of coming to the aid of descendants in time of trouble. The Greeks looked to their heroes, needless to say, for assistance in warfare and battle. When the battle of Salamis had been won, Themistocles declared that the Persians could never have been defeated without the intervention of Gods *and heroes,*[1] and after the battle of Marathon it was rumoured that Theseus, the national hero of Athens, had been seen fighting in person against the barbarians.[2] To their heroes the Greeks turned too for protection and support in personal calamity, sickness, and domestic crisis. But the functions of heroes were not specialized in any way and there was almost no strait or emergency which they might not be asked to meet. As Professor Nilsson puts it, 'they were good for everything'.[3] The heroes were indeed figures of great practical importance for the Greeks. Over and above these immediate and tangible needs, however, what in wider aspect were the aspirations which heroes and the heroized dead were called upon to satisfy, their former power conjoining with that of the Underworld? At this point our real difficulties begin, because what the vague and capacious term 'heroizing' indicates, as applied to the hero-reliefs, is that the partially deified main figure is conceived of as providing for his descendants an enlargement of life and strength whose full nature and scope we do not at all precisely know. The fundamental

[1] Herodotus, viii. 109.   [2] Plutarch, *Theseus,* 35.
[3] *Geschichte der Griechischen Religion* (2nd ed. 1955), vol. i, p. 716.

problem which the hero-reliefs present is to make out what pattern
of hopes and desires they reflect.

A number of the hero-reliefs are dominated by deeply interesting
representations of the snake-encircled tree. In a fourth-century
Thyrean relief (Pl. 4*a*), a youth feeds the snake coiled about the
tree in which his sword and shield are hanging, whilst his horse
paws the ground and a boy holds up his helmet towards him in
a gesture of adoration. In a Hellenistic relief from Pergamon
(Pl. 4*b*), the hero stands contemplatively in front of an altar at the
foot of the tree around which the snake is wreathed and pours
a libation. Beside him stands his consort, who joins with him in
pouring the wine. A lightly armoured attendant holds his horse,
and his dog looks up at him from in front of the altar. In a fourth-
century relief from the Piraeus (Pl. 4*c*) both the young rider,
assimilated to the figure of Dionysus, and his horse make obeisance
to the snake-encircled tree. On a relief of the Hellenistic period in
the local museum on Samos (Pl. 4*d*), the feasting hero holds up
a drinking horn to the snake, as it stretches down from the tree.
Next to him sits the consort-figure, and about him are grouped
various friends and attendants. Appearing from behind a wall we
see the head of the persistent horse, and, lying beneath the table, the
dog. I am convinced that the extraordinary power of these works of
art and the challenge to imaginative understanding which they
present have been insufficiently recognized. What kind of enrichment did the creators of these reliefs imagine as proceeding from the
snake-encircled tree to the hero and thence to themselves? And
why did they join tree and snake together in a single image? On
these critical and unavoidable questions, such historical antecedents
of the reliefs as have been suggested are more silent than the
sculptures themselves.

Jane Harrison discusses the last of these reliefs in her important
study of the origins of Greek religion, *Themis*, to which I owe Pl. 4*d*.
There has since been a certain reaction against the anthropological
approach to the history of ancient religious beliefs, and her work
has also fallen into disfavour with some scholars as being too
rhapsodic in tone and making too many risky inferences, although

the importance of the material to which she drew attention is not disputed. She maintains that the snake was originally a group totem image, embodying the vegetation-spirit, that the tree descends from a fertility cult no less ancient, and that both are 'symbols of life'. And very probably she is right. I am not concerned here with the correctness or otherwise of her theory, but rather with its extremely limited helpfulness. Miss Harrison has no difficulty in showing that Greek mythopœic and religious thought had as one of its aspects an extensive snake-syndrome. In the Minoan–Mycenaean religion, which preceded the Greek and from which it borrowed many of its ideas, the Snake-Goddess, whom we see represented by tiny bell-shaped Minoan figurines, encircled by snakes or holding one in each hand, was the object of a domestic cult carried on in houses and palaces.[1] Zeus in his aspects as 'The Gracious' (Meilichios) and 'The Acquirer' (Ktesios) was quite often represented as a snake.[2] The snake was also the sacred animal of Athena, appearing with her on a number of vase paintings, and, so Herodotus tells us, the Athenians believed that a huge snake lived in her temple as guardian of the Acropolis and sacrificed cakes to it once a month.[3] According to legend, the snake Python guarded the oracle of Delphi, until Apollo killed the snake and took over the oracle.[4] The 'Good Daimon' of domestic worship, to whom a libation was made at the end of a meal by pouring wine on the floor, was thought of as being a snake.[5] Cecrops, the legendary founder of Athens, was snake-formed in the lower part of his body.[6] And the Theban nobility were supposed to be descended from the armed men who sprang up when Cadmus killed the serpent guarding the spring of Ares and sowed its teeth in the ground.[7] We might make this list a considerably longer one. The overwhelming argument against doing so, it seems to me, is that adding instance to instance in this way sheds almost no light on the crucial meaning of the

[1] Nilsson, *M.M.R.*, pp. 321 ff.
[2] Nilsson, *Greek Popular Religion* (1940), pp. 67–70.
[3] Herodotus, viii. 41.   [4] Apollodorus, I. iv. 1.
[5] Nilsson, *Greek Popular Religion* (1940), p. 70.
[6] J. Harrison, *Themis* (1912), pp. 261 ff.
[7] Euripides, *Phoenissae*, 1006 ff.

snake, the burden of explanation and enhancement of understanding being merely referred from one fact to the next in a frustratingly circular way. Admittedly, we build up a rather more coherent general picture, because the snake on the hero-reliefs takes its place in a constellation of related facts, and there emerges a broad association with chthonian powers. But, as for the significance of the snake and the reason why it was felt to be so important, we move from the obscure to the no less obscure and do not begin to approach a solution.

We also find in Greek religious thought and practice a corresponding tree-syndrome. The cult of the tree was a central feature of the Minoan religion, as can be seen from the representation of the sacred tree on Minoan rings, where it stands behind a shrine or portal or is surrounded by dancing figures.[1] In the religious life of classical Greece the tree had a rather less pre-eminent but none the less very important place.[2] The laurel, the plane-tree, the tamarisk, and the apple-tree were sacred to Apollo, and some of his by-names are derived from them, the most famous of these being, of course, 'The Laurel-Bearer'.[3] Images of Apollo's twin sister Artemis, the most popular of the Greek goddesses, were wound about with willow, and she was given a by-name after this tree, as well as others after the chestnut and cedar.[4] A celebrated olive tree, sacred to the founder-hero Erectheus, stood in the Acropolis, which Herodotus tells us was burnt by the invading Persians, but on the next day was found to have brought forth a new shoot.[5] Other famous holy trees were Zeus' oak at Dodona, Heracles' wild olive-tree at Olympia, and Leto's palm tree on Delos. The carrying and use of branches played an important part in Greek rites and festive processions of all kinds.[6] And so we might go on. As with the snake, however, it soon becomes plain that the mounting instances are supplying us with little or no illumination, just as, when we work through Monsieur Perrot's fascinating collection of representations

[1] Nilsson, *M.M.R.*, pp. 262 ff.
[2] See Nilsson, *Geschichte der Griechischen Religion* (2nd ed., 1955), vol. ii, pp. 209 ff.
[3] Farnell, *Cults of the Greek States* (1907), vol. iv, p. 124.
[4] Nilsson, *Greek Popular Religion* (1940), p. 16.
[5] Herodotus, viii. 55. [6] Nilsson, *M.M.R.*, p. 264.

of the Babylonian sacred tree,[1] we find that no real entrée into the meaning of the central image is forthcoming, as he himself candidly and generously admits. In all probability the snake-encircled tree on the hero-reliefs is connected by devious lines of descent with the Minoan tree and snake motifs and with other later examples of these images, such as we have just mentioned, and in view of the increasing evidence of contacts between Greece and the Near East from Mycenaean times onwards we cannot rule out a contribution from this direction also. But, even if we could accurately piece together this genealogy, which we cannot do, we should only push back to where the visible records become more inscrutable, until eventually they disappear altogether, the central problem of why the snake and the tree took on major significance in the first place, what that significance was, and how these images were able to maintain their vitality for so long in the minds of the Greeks. Although no doubt from very early times both snake and tree had important associations with fertility, the notion of a primal fertility cult, so far from disposing of these problems, simply raises them over again in circumstances where our total ignorance makes them quite impossible to solve.

Indeed the very idea of fertility is one which easily misleads us into thinking we have got rid of problems which in fact we have scarcely begun to touch, and we must not allow ourselves to be bemused by it. We are apt to assume quite wrongly that archaic man must have had a clear and well-understood notion of fertility, and then have devised symbolic forms by which to represent it for magical and religious purposes, rather as we ourselves might proceed from our abstract notion of Justice to invent an allegorical figure standing for the same idea; that he started from a general conception and went on to clothe it, as it were, in symbolic draperies. But it is far more probable that he had no such conception, that thought and expression were inseparable, and that it was in the very execution of imaginative forms that early man first made real to himself his idea of what we loosely call 'fertility' and the nature of the cravings which he hoped that the powers associated

[1] Perrot, op. cit.

with the good things of the earth might satisfy. For, after man
became capable of producing images, it is most unlikely that he was
obsessed to the exclusion of all else by his primary need to ensure
a food supply, except perhaps in time of acute famine. Almost
certainly his will to live and interest in perpetuating his species had,
like ours, a deeply important imaginative dimension, his urge to
survive being inextricably bound up with more complex aspirations
and demands upon life. More often than not it is simply as a cover
for our very great ignorance of the real character of this vital element
in the life of the ancient world that we use such umbrella-phrases
as 'fertility-symbol', 'chthonian powers', 'vegetation spirit', and
others like them. Archaic man embodied his hopes of renewal and
fulfilment along with primary desires in forms and images associated
with fertility. In the same way, we can be sure, at a later time the
subtler elements in the Greek attitude to heroes were realized,
even for the Greeks themselves, mainly in the works of art by
which they represented them. And it is an illusion to suppose that,
provided we knew more about the background of the snake-
encircled trees on the hero-reliefs, we could restate the motives and
ideas underlying them in more sophisticated abstract terms. In
fact, if we only consider how dependent we ourselves are upon
imaginative forms for making articulate our own deep desires, it at
once becomes apparent that these productions already use the only
medium capable of expressing with exactness the very important
kind of thought which they do express, and that the task of understanding them is essentially an imaginative one.

When Miss Harrison comes to discuss why the tree and snake
were singled out from all other forms as being momentously
significant, her answers seem plainly insufficient. She suggests that
there was a kind of heritable fixation which was somehow passed
on from generation to generation. The tree must have acquired
sacred associations with life because of primitive man's intense
concern with food:

And of these fruits, before cereals came in with settled agriculture,
most conspicuous and arresting would be the fruits of wild trees. The

fruit-growing tree would be sacred, and its sanctity would quickly pass to other trees.[1]

The snake's death-associations are accounted for thus:

> It is not hard to see reasons why a snake should be associated with a dead man. The snake is an uncanny beast gliding in and out of holes in the earth. He may well have been seen haunting old tombs.[2]

No explanation is offered apart from general chthonian associations of why it was chosen to function as a daimon of life. But there is no reason for denigrating the intelligence and imagination of early civilizations in this way. The fifteenth-century Italian humanist, Pico della Mirandola[3] (1463–94), writing in the belief that the earliest sages and artists possessed a kind of pristine wisdom or imaginative insight and devised images so as to express it, is far more just and plausible here:

> The ancient fathers could not have represented one image by another had they not known the hidden affinities and harmonies of the universe. Otherwise there would not have been any reason whatever why they should have represented a thing by one image rather than by an opposite one.[4]

Whatever reservations we may have about the hidden 'harmonies of the universe', he is plainly right to press the question Miss Harrison avoids: why one image was chosen and not another.

Largely for reasons already indicated, I have found it unrewarding to approach this question by gathering more anthropological data of the kind Miss Harrison relies on. Indeed I believe the intriguing arcana of ritual and folk-lore to be a side-track that takes us away from the central problem, as does too large an apparatus of comparative symbolism. There is no end to inventorying other

---

[1] Harrison, op. cit., p. 167.   [2] Ibid., p. 268.
[3] An account (with bibliography) of this extraordinary man who at twenty-three offered to defend nine hundred theses in Rome against all comers, will be found in P. O. Kristeller, *Eight Philosophers of the Italian Renaissance* (1965).
[4] *Heptaplus*, ed. E. Garin (1942), p. 192. I owe this reference to E. H. Gombrich's 'Icones Symbolicae. The Visual Image in Neo-Platonic Thought', *J.W.C.I.* xi (1948).

people's employments of an image, and we are liable in the process both to erect a barrier between ourselves and its immediate force and to be deflected from the task of understanding the pattern of thought and feeling from which it derives its significance and vitality. Yeats makes the essential point by saying that we are furthest from symbols when we are most busy.[1] But this does not mean that we have to depend upon special states of mind affording occult knowledge, such as the forbidding *ekstasis* or *furor* by which the Neoplatonists held that the visible world has to be penetrated, because there are sources of illumination which are not in any way remote or esoteric. In the first place we should on no account neglect our present untheoretical response to the constituent elements of the image we are considering. 'A fool sees not the same tree that a wise man sees.' Assuredly the first step towards understanding the tree and the snake *is to look at them,*[2] and one living tree or a single snake, attentively regarded, will serve us better than volumes of information about their respective cults. To illustrate the level of simple-mindedness I envisage at this stage, take first the tree. It is the most long-surviving and stable of living things, though vulnerable and subservient to man, wholly predictable in its changes, a calendar whereon we may read the sure progress of the seasons, constant in formal outline from year to year, a landmark. It might stand in a churchyard, for it has associations which reach towards the idea of Eternity, yet not too far away from the security of the institutional fold; and it might mark the site of one such 'dear familiar place' as that in which Yeats's laurel tree is rooted. Our reactions to the snake are certain to be as towards a contrary and antitype of the tree. The snake is the most inconstant and unpredictable in formal outline of living things and approaches the verge of amorphousness. Far more than the monster of imagination, with which it shares this last characteristic, it is alert and mobile. It is elusive and keeps no sure domicile. Watching a snake involves a second-to-second uncertainty where its head will turn next and you cannot look it straight between the eyes. The snake is an

[1] In his essay, 'The Symbolism of Poetry'.
[2] The reptile house at the zoo should not be forgotten in this connection.

extraordinarily open structure in the sense that no possible direction of movement seems at any moment to be closed to any part of it. Handling a snake evokes feelings and symptoms of an elementary kind hard to specify but unmistakably alien to established habits and concerns. All this is encompassed in the precise Sumerian phrase 'the snake who knows no charm'. Although Kramer interprets this as meaning simply that it was immune to the spells of priests, the idea of the snake is one we feel to harbour something inimical to the permanence of all our designs upon nature: techniques, boundaries, moral systems, institutions, and even language itself. We need to begin by identifying whatever in ourselves responds to and finds expression in such primary characteristics of tree and snake respectively.

But for deeper insight into the meaning of the snake-encircled tree and its relationship to the ideal enclave we have mainly to depend upon a handful of Renaissance painters and poets who, applying themselves to the elements within the human mind which this image sets forth and devising yet subtler forms whereby to present them, advanced the frontier of understanding and permanently enriched the imaginative life of man.

PART TWO

TOWARDS AN INTERPRETATION

3

THEMES IN RENAISSANCE ART AND LITERATURE

WE shall now compare two of the very greatest treatments of ideal landscape in Renaissance art and the three most important plays of Shakespeare's final period. With the consideration of Shakespeare's last plays, to which most of this chapter is devoted, the interpretative stage of our inquiry begins.

I. PRIMAVERA

Botticelli's *Primavera* (Pl. 5) is one of two or three paintings which represent for most of us in its quintessence the recovery during the Quattrocento in their pristine form of those earlier pagan gods who had so tenaciously survived through many metamorphoses, their innate strength conspiring with the mind's resistance at all times to any attempt to reform its entire apparatus. The principal impression which the picture makes upon us is well conveyed by Jean Seznec, commenting on the art of Botticelli's period in general:

It is indeed worthy of note that during the most radiant period of the Renaissance, the iconographical types that had been 'handed down', and therefore altered, were almost everywhere abandoned in favor of types 'rediscovered' in their primal purity. It is also significant that during the same period there seems to be an interruption in the mythographical tradition, at least in Italy (no Italian history of the gods appeared between Boccaccio and Giraldi). It is as if nothing more was now needed, in order to know and understand the gods, than to look out at the surrounding world and listen to the voice of instinct; as if man had at last penetrated to the inner meaning of mythology, now that he was engaged in rehabilitating, along with physical beauty, the realm of nature and the flesh.[1]

The complex subject of *Primavera* raises deeply interesting problems. With one reservation, I shall accept most of Professor Wind's brilliant analysis of the picture in *Pagan Mysteries in the Renaissance* (1958), and then part company with it over the crucial question of Mercury's role in the painting. Its setting is an idealized glade, presided over by Venus in the peaceable restraining aspect attributed to her by Neoplatonic thought, and Vasari records that the painting 'signifies spring'. According to Wind, on the right of the picture we have the transformation of the nymph Chloris into Flora under the assault of Zephyr, the spring wind, described in Ovid's account of the festival of the flower-goddess.[2] The three Graces on the left side of the picture identify themselves as Chastity, Beauty, and Pleasure. And Pico della Mirandola declares that 'the unity of Venus is unfolded in the trinity of the Graces'.[3] They are performing a dance of initiation and the two lateral Graces, Beauty and Pleasure, gently raising their hands over the head of Chastity, are admitting her into the mystery of Love, as Cupid aims his arrow with deadly accuracy at her head. With a generous sweep of her left arm, Beauty touches hands with Pleasure whilst she clasps the hand of Chastity with the other. And so there arises between the figures a kind of dialectic in which Chastity is lent the qualities she lacks by the two initiating Graces and imparts to them in return something of her own restraint. At the left of the picture Mercury (Pl. 5*a*), escort of souls, patron of metaphysicians, merchants, and thieves, toys with a band of clouds, lifting his snake-staff to touch them (Pl. 5*b*). Such in outline is Wind's analysis. To set it in proper perspective, however, we need to take into account one most relevant fact which he does not mention. Wind assumes that the presence of the Graces in the picture requires to be explained, unlike that of the triad of figures on the right of the painting, which, he says, 'derive from a passage in Ovid'.[4] But in

---

[1] *The Survival of the Pagan Gods* (1953), p. 320.   [2] *Fasti*, v. 183 ff.
[3] *Conclusiones . . . de modo intelligendi hymnos Orphei*, No. 8.
[4] 'It is legitimate, therefore, to inquire how the triad of figures on the right of the

Plate 5. Botticelli: *Primavera (Florence, Uffizi Gallery)*

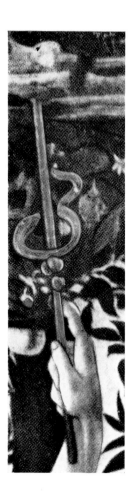

Plate 5a. Mercury, *from Primavera*

Plate 5b. Caduceus of Mercury and band of cloud, from *Primavera*

fact the appearance of the Graces provides the climax of the episode of Chloris' transformation into Flora, as Ovid describes it. The first thing to look at if we want help in understanding *Primavera* is the poetry which inspired it:

> I was Chloris, a nymph of the happy fields where, as you have heard, dwelt fortunate men of old. It would be immodest to describe my figure, but it won me the hand of a god. It was spring and I was wandering; Zephyr caught sight of me and I slipped away; he came after me and I fled; but he was the stronger, and Boreas had given his brother the full right to rape by daring to carry off the daughter of Erechtheus from his house as a prize. But he atoned for his violence by making me his bride, and my marriage-bed gives me nothing to complain of; I enjoy spring at all times; ever abundant is the year; ever the tree is clothed with leaves and the earth with pasture. I have a fertile garden in the fields that are my dowry, fanned by the breeze and fed by a spring of running water. My husband filled this garden with delicate flowers and said to me, 'Goddess, be queen of flowers.' I have often wanted to count the colours spread there, but could not, for their number was past counting. As soon as the dewy hoar-frost has been shaken from the leaves and all the varied foliage has been warmed by the sun's rays, the Hours assemble, elaborately dressed, and gather my gifts into light baskets. Immediately the Graces approach, and twine garlands and wreaths to bind their heavenly hair.[1]

The prime reason why *Primavera* has its spring-theme, its Graces, and its marvellous carpet of flowers is the same: they are all in Ovid's poem. This does not in any way disprove Wind's explanation or make it less than deeply illuminating, but it does indicate that the inspiration of Botticelli's painting was probably rather more poetic and rather less philosophical than he suggests.

Professor Wind's account of Mercury is so important that it must

painting, which derive from a passage in Ovid, is related to the formal triad of the Graces on the left, and whether these two contrasting groups, being placed on either side of Venus, perhaps represent two consecutive phases of one coherent theory of love.' Op. cit., p. 101. Wind nowhere indicates that the Graces are in Botticelli's source. Their presence there would point to the inclusion of Mercury, who is traditionally, as Wind observes, leader of the Graces.

[1] *Fasti*, v. 197–220.

be given in his own words. After describing the status which Mercury enjoyed in Renaissance thought as the supremely ingenious god, the revealer of things hidden, and pointing out that Boccaccio ascribed to him a specific power to dispel mental clouds, he writes:

> Even so, one may doubt whether Mercury's concern with clouds is to be understood in the *Primavera* entirely in a negative sense, as if he were purging the mind or the air of an obstruction. For that his gaze is too contemplative, his bearing too poetical. He plays with the clouds rather as a Platonic hierophant, touching them but lightly because they are the beneficent veils through which the splendour of transcendent truth may reach the beholder without destroying him. To 'reveal the mysteries' is to move the veils while preserving their dimness, so that the truth may penetrate but not glare. The transcendent secret is kept hidden, yet made to transpire through the disguise. 'Nec mysteria quae non occulta', wrote Pico in the *Heptaplus*; or, in his Commentary on Benivieni's *Amore*: 'Divine things must be concealed under enigmatic veils and poetic dissimulation.' As an *interpres secretorum* (Boccaccio's phrase for Mercury), Mercury looks upward and touches the clouds. 'Summus animae ad Deum ascendentis gradus caligo dicitur atque lumen.' The highest wisdom is to know that the divine light resides in clouds.[1]

And Wind goes on to argue that we see in *Primavera* a three-fold Neoplatonic pattern of procession, conversion, and return. The Invisible enters the sensible world as wind or spirit in the passion of Zephyr, is converted in the dance of the Graces, and returns to itself through the averted figure of Mercury, who points to the Beyond.

Is Wind's interpretation of Mercury's role in the painting a truly satisfying one? It has, surely, one serious drawback. He gives examples in which Mercury is represented as penetrating or dispelling clouds, but it seems quite uncharacteristic of this most volatile god, even if in theory a natural extension of his mediating function, that he should *wait upon* a veil of cloud, preserving dimness yet filtering the transcendent. No precedent is given for him in this incongruous role and it does not suit the extreme nonchalance of

---

[1] Wind, op. cit., p. 107.

his stance and gesture. At this critical point Wind's explanation seems strained and at odds with the impression we receive from the picture, and it is essential that an analysis of *Primavera* should convincingly accommodate the contained negligence of Mercury's bearing and attitude, together with our sense of its exact appropriateness. Furthermore it is in another respect incomplete, because no account of why Mercury is skimming a band of cloud with his snake-staff in so densely symbolic a painting can be entirely satisfactory if it altogether passes over the significance and imaginative force of the caduceus itself in relation to the god, the clouds towards which he directs his gaze, and the total subject. In the interpretation of Shakespeare's last plays which now follows, I seek amongst other things to establish the case for a rather different view of Mercury's role in *Primavera*, one which does justice, I believe, both to the collected insouciance of the god and to the meaning of his wand in the context of the picture as a whole.

II. SHAKESPEARE'S FINAL PERIOD

In the great plays of his final period, Shakespeare turned to ideal forms which present those contrary modes of fulfilment whose reconciliation has ever been the central task both of the poet and of the imaginative life common to all men. Since abstract equivalents are here a weak and imprecise substitute for poetry and art, it will be enough for the moment to say that they correspond to man's perpetual craving for the infinitely various and his need for the sure domicile of a continuing order. And the fact that these human ends are opposed to one another constitutes, as we shall see, a dilemma of the most fundamental kind, a problem which Blake was to express some two hundred years later when he inscribed at the top of a sketch for his *Ancient of Days*[1] the question (and protest) 'Who shall bind the Infinite?' Now we must consider *Antony and Cleopatra*, *The Winter's Tale*, and *The Tempest*. In their poetic aspect, even though one is a tragedy and the other two are so-called romances, these plays, as I shall try to show, set forth different facets of a

[1] Blake's Notebook (the Rossetti MS.), p. 96.

single composite theme and form in effect a trilogy; and Coleridge's suggestion that *Antony and Cleopatra* rivals the four acknowledged major tragedies 'in all exhibitions of a giant power' applies still more forcibly to the triad of which it is a member.

A. *Antony and Cleopatra*

By opening the play with a clash of opinion over the value of boundaries, limits, and restraints, Shakespeare prefigures the main poetic theme he will develop more explicitly than in any other of his first scenes. The exposition is diagrammatically simple and formal. First we have Philo's blunt unmetaphysical complaint, heard only by the audience, that his master by breaking with temper and due limit has allowed the heroic frame to disintegrate:

> Nay, but this dotage of our general's
> O'erflows the measure: those his goodly eyes
> That o'er the files and musters of the war
> Have glow'd like plated Mars, now bend, now turn
> The office and devotion of their view
> Upon a tawny front. His captain's heart,
> Which in the scuffles of great fights hath burst
> The buckles on his breast, reneges all temper,
> And is become the bellows and the fan
> To cool a gipsy's lust.

Plainly a great soldier with the world at his feet has abandoned the discipline that secures resilience and achievement. There follows instantly the assertion of quite another ideal:

CLEOPATRA. If it be love indeed, tell me how much.
ANTONY. There's beggary in the love that can be reckon'd.
CLEOPATRA. I'll set a bourn how far to be belov'd.
ANTONY. Then must thou needs find out new heaven, new earth.

It is pauperdom to settle for a satisfaction that falls short of being boundless and measureless. All is the only cry for man. The placing of the main stresses—múch, reckóned, bóurn—in itself tells against love being the real subject of this last exchange. Philo's argument and that of the royal couple are, essentially, different prescriptions

Plate 6a. Botticelli: *The Birth of Venus (Florence, Uffizi Gallery)*
Plate 6b. Venus goes to the Lover's aid: fifteenth-century MS. of Roman
de la Rose (*Bodleian Library, MS. Douce 195*)

Plate 7a. The Castle of Jealousy

Plate 7b. Venus surprises the Castle of Jealousy: fifteenth-century MS. of Roman de la Rose
(*Bodleian Library*, *MS. Douce 195*)

for fulfilment, and also by implication different answers to the question, 'Who shall bind the Infinite?' The messenger who now brings news from Rome gains no hearing and is brushed aside by Antony with a comprehensive dismissal of the whole system of interlocking purposes and expectations he represents:

> Let Rome in Tiber melt, and the wide arch
> Of the rang'd empire fall! Here is my space,
> Kingdoms are clay: our dungy earth alike
> Feeds beast as man.

The greatest sphere of worldly power is an oppressive little allot-ment in nature's sleepy inert domain, cozening the soul by its deceptive physical mass and scale. Mockingly proposing a session with diplomats as a lively evening's diversion, Cleopatra wins from Antony the first of many tributes to her supremacy in the art of making wantonness and caprice delectable. Then the lovers make their first counter-bid to the satisfaction of holding and manipula-ting the destiny of half the world:

> To-night we'll wander through the streets and note
> The qualities of people. Come, my queen . . .

To join incognito the random movement of the night crowd, as with no set purpose unchartable promptings shift it minute by minute into one configuration, and then another.

There is nothing in the least arbitrary about the choice here of this particular 'surfeited pastime' rather than another, any more than there is about Cleopatra's decision a little later to make an expedition to the riverside:

> Give me mine angle, we'll to the river: there,
> My music playing far off, I will betray
> Tawny-finn'd fishes.

For the poetic theme of *Antony and Cleopatra* is the marginal, the extreme verge of the formed world, and to confirm this essential point in a preliminary way we need only recall a few lines, all of them spoken by Cleopatra, in which is plainly recognizable a compression of poetic energy not met before in Shakespeare's verse:

O sun,
Burn the great sphere thou mov'st in: darkling stand
The varying shore o' the world.

The crown o' th' earth doth melt.

the odds is gone,
And there is nothing left remarkable
Beneath the visiting moon.

his delights
Were dolphin-like, they show'd his back above
The element they lived in. . . .

The darkening shore, the determining centre of the world dissolved, the obliteration of all that gives distinction and difference, so that the moon must look in vain for anything to invest with mystery, abundance surfacing from its containing medium—all this poetry has for its basic idea, not a particular bounding line, but in widest conceivable terms the border between the formed and the formless, that alien region with which a great part of the poetry of the last plays occupies itself.

The story which Shakespeare inherited from Plutarch in North's translation harboured the embryo of this very theme. Plutarch tells how, on her journey down the river Cydnus to meet Antonius, Cleopatra identified herself with the goddess Venus:

She was layed under a pavillion of cloth of gold of tissue, apparelled and attired like the goddesse Venus, commonly drawen in picture: and hard by her, on either hand of her, pretie faire boyes apparelled as painters doe set forth god Cupide, with little fannes in their hands, with the which they fanned wind upon her.

This passage, as all students of the play know, Shakespeare largely transliterated in his celebrated description of Cleopatra's first encounter with Antony:

ENOBARBUS.   I will tell you.
The barge she sat in, like a burnish'd throne,
Burn'd on the water: the poop was beaten gold;
Purple the sails, and so perfumed that
The winds were love-sick with them; the oars were silver,

Which to the tune of flutes kept stroke, and made
The water which they beat to follow faster,
As amorous of their strokes. For her own person,
It beggar'd all description: she did lie
In her pavilion, cloth-of-gold, of tissue,
O'er-picturing that Venus where we see
The fancy outwork nature: on each side her
Stood pretty dimpled boys, like smiling Cupids,
With divers-colour'd fans, whose wind did seem
To glow the delicate cheeks which they did cool,
And what they undid did.
AGRIPPA.   O, rare for Antony!
ENOBARBUS. Her gentlewomen, like the Nereides,
So many mermaids, tended her i' th' eyes,
And made their bends adornings. At the helm
A seeming mermaid steers: the silken tackle
Swell with the touches of those flower-soft hands,
That yarely frame the office. From the barge
A strange invisible perfume hits the sense
Of the adjacent wharfs. The city cast
Her people out upon her; and Antony,
Enthron'd i' the market place, did sit alone,
Whistling to th' air; which, but for vacancy,
Had gone to gaze on Cleopatra too,
And made a gap in nature.

In this justly famous passage Enobarbus declares that Cleopatra
vied with the finest pictorial realizations of Venus and eclipsed
them, as her barge lay off the bank of the river. And it is specifically
in the moment of nearing the shore that Venus Anadyomene has
at all times most poignantly haunted imagination, as we see in
Botticelli's great picture (Pl. 6*a*), in illuminated manuscripts of
romance literature (Pl. 6*b*), as well as in the earliest poetic treatment:

First she came near to holy Cythera, then reached Cyprus, the land
surrounded by sea. Then she stepped out a goddess, tender and
beautiful, and round her slender feet the green grass shot up.

Thus Hesiod in the *Theogony*.[1] 'So landete die Göttin': this short bare statement expresses the heart of Rilke's poem *Birth of Venus*. Aphrodite in her most potent impact on the mind, and so on art, is essentially a creature of the margin between sea and land, and in imitating her Cleopatra associates herself with this aspect of the goddess.

Furthermore, the climax of Plutarch's narrative turns, of course, upon Cleopatra's experimental interest in snakes and the asp which vanishes mysteriously leaving no trace of itself except some marks in the sand. And this element in Plutarch's story Shakespeare expanded and developed into his poetic conception of the 'serpent of old Nile'. At this point we re-establish contact with our Sumerian myth and with our preliminary observations on the snake's main characteristics in Chapter One, where it was suggested that the idea of the snake represents for us the periphery of the known system and is felt to be inimical to all permanent forms. Cleopatra's overriding motive and rule of life, as Shakespeare presents her, is to be in all things wanton (O.E. *wan* = un/*togen*, pp. of *teon*[2] = to discipline), never to commit herself, to accept no containing limits and elude every species of confinement, so that in simple logic life holds but one ultimate horror for her, captivity, and the device that epitomizes the whole idea of captivity, the trap.

> O infinite virtue, com'st thou smiling from
> The world's great snare uncaught?

is her unforgettable greeting when Antony returns from his first and last successful engagement in the final battle. To revert to the exact and pregnant poetic epithet applied to the snake in the Sumerian myth *Gilgamesh and the Huluppu-Tree*, the 'serpent of old Nile' has made it her *raison d'être* and dominant principle to 'know no charm'. And her proper domain is the outermost margin of the formed order which the snake represents, the 'varying shore of the world'.

Cleopatra, we are told, is limitlessly various, but it is not primarily in her human relationships or actual behaviour that this

---

[1] 192 ff.   [2] Probably cognate with *teohan* = to bind or tie.

'infinite variety' presents itself, although we see her cunningly releasing Antony but implanting her image in his mind, threatening to give her hand-maiden 'bloody teeth', haling a messenger up and down by the hair, showing an uninhibited and diverse vitality, and we hear how she once had herself carried to Caesar in a mattress, how on another occasion she hopped 'forty paces through the public street'. We accept these vagaries as being samples from a boundless repertoire, however, mainly because of her power to express herself in transcendent poetry, which makes us realize that, but for his experience of such overwhelming energies as are displayed there, man would not have needed to distinguish gods and their operations from other elements in his life. Its most wonderful exhibitions are concentrated in the final part of the play, after Antony's bungled suicide and death. When the confused episode at the monument is over, Antony speaks his dignified Roman farewell. Cleopatra gives rein to an unmitigated self-concern in the horrifying question,

> Noblest of men, woo't die?
> Hast thou no care of me?

Antony dies. And then follows in an astonishing modulation into an elegiac and universal mode of speech, the incandescence of

> O wither'd is the garland of the war,
> The soldier's pole is fall'n: young boys and girls
> Are level now with men; the odds is gone,
> And there is nothing left remarkable
> Beneath the visiting moon.

In an instant, having struggled to the very end to find a remitting alternative, she confronts and holds before herself the truth: that the lamp is out and all that might significantly separate one object from another extinct. We realize at this moment that her treacheries and lies, her elevation of *mauvaise foi* into an ideal, her evasion of the least consistency tying her to past loyalty or future policy, as well as conserving her strength, have kept intact the immediate access to present truth and capacity for sudden knowledge that make up her peculiar genius.

What is the price of experience? Do men buy it for a song?
Or wisdom for a dance in the street? No, it is bought with the price
Of all that a man hath, his house, his wife, his children.
Wisdom is sold in the desolate market where none come to buy,
And in the wither'd field where the farmer plows for bread in vain.

Thus Blake on knowledge through experience. Cleopatra commands swift certitude of another kind, for never having let herself become involved in experience or immeshed in any kind of commitment whatsoever, she has no need to untrammel and disengage herself from the constricting toils of either. Essentially, it is the knowledge of innocence. And at the end it will earn for the 'triple-turned whore' a strangely moving tribute to this her most paradoxical quality, when the attendant Charmian stoops over the body of her mistress and speaks the simple elegy,

> Now boast thee, death, in thy possession lies
> A lass unparallel'd.

The moment of truth which follows the death of Antony turns Cleopatra into a profoundly dangerous opponent, and not simply because her unfailing opportunism is lent a razor edge by pride and despair. She has discovered in herself a majestic objectivity and constancy of purpose, which express themselves as she rallies her shaken and fearful gentlewomen:

> All's but naught.
> Patience is sottish, and impatience does
> Become a dog that's mad: then is it sin
> To rush into the secret house of death
> Ere death dare come to us? How do you, women?
> What, what, good cheer! Why, how now, Charmian?
> My noble girls! Ah, women, women, look,
> Our lamp is spent, it's out. Good sirs, take heart:
> We'll bury him; and then, what's brave, what's noble,
> Let's do't after the high Roman fashion,
> And make death proud to take us. Come, away.
> This case of that huge spirit now is cold.
> Ah, women, women! Come; we have no friend
> But resolution, and the briefest end.

Moreover, a new factor has begun to operate alongside and in conjunction with Cleopatra's dread of being carried in triumph through the streets of Rome, and the cunning which makes it axiomatic for her to outwit Octavius if she possibly can. Now the same immense drives that sustained her passion for Antony are channelled towards death with terrible intensity, because to dismantle physical form itself as an intolerable confine, to escape the final horror of captivity by ruining the fabric of 'this mortal house', to repay the tyranny of circumstance in its own coin, has taken on the value of all that Antony once signified and satisfies the same principle:

> My desolation does begin to make
> A better life. 'Tis paltry to be Caesar:
> Not being Fortune, he's but Fortune's knave,
> A minister of her will: and it is great
> To do that thing that ends all other deeds,
> Which shackles accidents and bolts up change;
> Which sleeps, and never palates more the dung,
> The beggar's nurse, and Caesar's.

In the next respite from playing with consummate skill her last hand against Caesar, Cleopatra turns in a passage of critical importance away from Antony himself towards what he represented for her:

CLEOPATRA. I dreamt there was an Emperor Antony.
    O such another sleep, that I might see
    But such another man!
DOLABELLA. If it might please ye—
CLEOPATRA. His face was as the heavens: and therein stuck
    A sun and moon, which kept their course, and lighted
    The little O, the earth.
DOLABELLA. Most sovereign creature—
CLEOPATRA. His legs bestrid the ocean: his rear'd arm
    Crested the world: his voice was propertied
    As all the tuned spheres, and that to friends;
    But when he meant to quail and shake the orb,
    He was as rattling thunder. For his bounty,

> There was no winter in't; an autumn 'twas
> That grew the more by reaping: his delights
> Were dolphin-like, they show'd his back above
> The element they lived in: in his livery
> Walk'd crowns and crownets; realms and islands were
> As plates dropp'd from his pocket.
> DOLABELLA. Cleopatra!
> CLEOPATRA. Think you there was, or might be, such a man
> As this I dreamed of?
> DOLABELLA. Gentle madam, no.
> CLEOPATRA. You lie, up to the hearing of the gods.
> But, if there be, or ever were, one such,
> It's past the size of dreaming: nature wants stuff
> To vie strange forms with fancy; yet, to imagine
> An Antony, were nature's piece 'gainst fancy,
> Condemning shadows quite.

Antony had signified for her abundance without the oppressiveness of autumnal finality, a life that is ever breaking from its confining element, substantial power spilling over from childlike abandon. She declares, with the uneasy violence which she reserves for the assertion of what she knows to be false, that this Antony was the work of nature, a piece of reality dwarfing the world of fantasies and dreams; but more important than her conclusion is the question she asks, which opens a distinction between the ideal form she has projected upon her lover and the man himself. 'If we think that it is the beloved whom we really love', observes La Rochefoucauld, 'we are much deceived.' And fundamentally Cleopatra does not deceive herself. She demands to know, not whether there has ever been a historical Antony, but whether the physical universe has contained, or could contain, *her* Antony, the god-like figure of her imagination. The capacity to make this crucial separation at such a moment is a measure of her energy and innate strength, and the alien awareness and self-sufficiency it reveals, felt as a threat to our deep affections of relegation to the ancillary and dispensable, must surely have contributed to those irrelevant charges of immorality levelled against Cleopatra and against the play at various times.

Now that Antony is dead, the defiance of the limited and the finite that he once stood for can only be realized in self-destruction.

A number of Shakespeare's readers have found something self-deceiving and unreal in Cleopatra's wonderful description of the asp which gives her liberty,

> Peace, peace!
> Dost thou not see my baby at my breast,
> That sucks the nurse asleep?

But the image she uses here is poetically exact and springs from her direct knowledge of herself. It develops the basic idea of the invitation she has just addressed to the snake,

> Come, thou mortal wretch,
> With thy sharp teeth this knot intrinsicate
> Of life at once untie. . . .

The snake is not only an agent of death: a part of the formed world yet at enmity with form and its boundaries, it here unlooses for good the figured complex which is the foundation of the binder's skill and brings release. And in the human sphere, the nearest counterpart to the snake is the child, the most open and un-committed representative of our species, a creature for whom all possibilities are still intact. Considered in their imaginative aspect, young children and snakes are cousins beneath the skin, living things for whom every development is entertainable. Not only has the child, unlike ourselves, an indeterminable range of possible lives before it, but as with the snake, you cannot predict from moment to moment where it will move or what it will do next. Children and snakes are in their respective classes infinitely various creatures *par excellence*, and with this association between them we shall shortly have to concern ourselves further.[1] In drawing the asp to her breast and likening it to a baby, Cleopatra realizes poetically and dramatically the snake-like and childlike principle in herself, to which she remains faithful even at the price of being faithless to everything else.

[1] I reserve various illustrations of this connection, which seems to me to be intuitably plain, until the next Section, where they are still more in point than here.

Cleopatra's identification of snake with child, and of herself with
both, springs, we have said, from her self-awareness and essential
truthfulness. And at first this may seem difficult to reconcile with
the unconvincing parade of the idea of reunion after death in her
final speech: Antony, as audience to her act, as her destination, as
liable to bestow his first kiss on Iras if she procrastinates. But I do not
think that it is in fact so. We can tell that these relatively inert
lines are secondary, partly because no one remembers them, but
also because Cleopatra herself relegates the idea of reunion to the
status of a belief:

> Methinks I hear
> Antony call: I see him rouse himself
> To praise my noble act.

The 'serpent of old Nile' has no use for credence except to apply it
to the fundamentally suspect. The poetic core of her last words, on
the other hand, is immune from theatricality and self-deception.
Just before he dies, Antony lyricizes in mild euphoric vein on his
future condition:

> Where souls do couch on flowers, we'll hand in hand,
> And with our sprightly port make the ghosts gaze:
> Dido and her Aeneas shall want troops,
> And all the haunt be ours.

Contrast with these lines the adamant of

> I have
> Immortal longings in me.

And

> I am fire and air: my other elements
> I give to baser life.

This is the truth, neither more nor less.

As well as realizing the marginal extreme as Cleopatra's domain
by identifying her poetically and dramatically with the snake, and
in other ways that we have mentioned, Shakespeare supports this

poetic conception by an abundance of ancillary images, principally
through continual emphasis upon dissolution and dissolving forms:

>   as it determines,
> So dissolve my life.
>
> That which is now a horse even with a thought
> The wrack dislimns, and makes it indistinct
> As water is in water.
>
> Dissolve, thick cloud, and rain, that I may say,
> The gods themselves do weep!

He further strengthens it by associating Cleopatra with elusive and
peripheral creatures:

> To this great fairy I'll commend thy acts,
> Make her thanks bless thee.
>
>   My nightingale,
> We have beat them to their beds.

And by the numerous references to the banks of the Nile and to
fishing, a theme which asserts itself without incongruity even at
the tragic moment when Cleopatra hauls up her dying lover into
the monument:

> Here's sport indeed! How heavy weighs my lord!

The play is full too of images that evoke a sense of the continually
shifting, the merging, and the indeterminate: cloud, water, rain,
showers, vapour, 'the morn-dew on the myrtle-leaf'. And all this
imagery suggests the outermost verge of the formed order. Furthermore, if we trust our reaction to Cleopatra, as Shakespeare conceives
her, to the infinitely various marginal region which is her proper
territory, and to the central image of the snake which embraces
both, we see that they represent for us, as they do for Antony, a
persistent ideal of the very greatest importance, which we are at no
price ready to forfeit or renounce. At the same time we cannot but
feel that this ideal is somehow one-sided and incomplete, and in the
next Section I shall try to bring out more clearly why this is so.

Not only did Plutarch provide the seminal idea from which
Shakespeare developed his interpretation of Cleopatra; he also

invested the figure of her lover and victim with a mythopœic significance which Shakespeare likewise took over and realized on a larger scale, presenting in his story of the ruin of Antonius far more than a picture of the soldier-hero in decline. One of a family supposedly descended from the god Hercules, his expression 'as is commonly seen in Hercules' pictures', Antonius by his disintegration implicates in wider aspect the heroic idea itself. And Plutarch emphasizes this by recording how, on the eve of Antonius' final defeat, the city of Alexandria and its god-like protector were mysteriously subverted from within, when Dionysiac music was suddenly heard, as if an invisible rout were moving in satyr-like dance through the streets and out of the gate towards the enemy:

Furthermore, the selfe same night within litle of midnight, when all the citie was quiet, full of feare and sorrowe, thinking what would be the issue and ende of this warre: it is said that sodainly they heard a marvelous sweete harmonie of sundrie sortes of instrumentes of musicke, with the crie of a multitude of people, as they had bene dauncing, and had song as they use in Bacchus feastes, with movinges and turnings after the maner of the Satyres: and it seemed that this daunce went through the city unto the gate that opened to the enemies, and that all the troupe that made this noise they heard, went out of the city at that gate. Now, such as in reason sought the depth of the interpretacion of this wonder, thought that it was the god unto whom Antonius bare singulare devotion to counterfeate and resemble him, that did forsake them.

Shakespeare retains the episode but gives it sparely, almost perfunctorily:

> [*music of the hautboys as under the stage*]
> SECOND SOLDIER. Peace! what noise?
> FIRST SOLDIER. List, list!
> SECOND SOLDIER. Hark!
> FIRST SOLDIER. Music i' the air.
> THIRD SOLDIER. Under the earth.
> FOURTH SOLDIER. It signs well, does it not?
> THIRD SOLDIER. No.

FIRST SOLDIER. Peace, I say!
    What should this mean?
SECOND SOLDIER. 'Tis the god Hercules, whom Antony lov'd
    Now leaves him.
FIRST SOLDIER. Walk: let's see if other watchmen
    Do hear what we do.

The reason for this economy is plain. In his whole presentation of Antony and his fate, Shakespeare has appropriated and transformed into poetic drama the underlying idea of subversion by a principle opposed to the very notion of a hero.

Shakespeare's Antony seeks in his love for Cleopatra the satisfaction without limits which he craves. Enobarbus divines the essential point:

> Age cannot wither her, nor custom stale
> Her infinite variety: other women cloy
> The appetites they feed: but she makes hungry
> Where most she satisfies.

It is the perennial quest, under one guise after another, for an object that will never justify weariness. Pursuing this unlimited enrichment of his life, he is utterly destroyed. A clumsy intruder in the region of the marginal which is Cleopatra's element, his fortitude and resolution were fashioned for every extremity except that he sets himself to contain, the one force calculated to weaken and dissolve his strength. He needs Cleopatra's world, and yet it is no place for him. His judgement is imperceptibly eroded and undermined; he allows himself the fatal indulgence of fighting Octavius on the treacherous sea, when he has an overwhelming superiority by land; and in the final moment of crisis, outmanœuvred and betrayed from within as from without, he can only withdraw his mind hopelessly from the military realities. But Shakespeare also sets forth the ruin of Antony as being of more far-reaching consequence than any single personal calamity. With him falls too a great conception. For it belongs to the very idea of a hero that in confronting mischance he shall not be vulnerable from an unlimited number of directions. In some ways at least the cards must be

stacked in his favour. The aged Lear, who has endured so much that
he usurps his life, retains to the end enough strength to kill the
slave who is hanging Cordelia. Hamlet has the technique to win at
the odds in the fencing match. 'Absent thee from felicity awhile /
And in this harsh world draw thy breath in pain / To tell my story.'
The tragic hero expects and usually obtains some complicity from
the society that creates him in maintaining the ideal form he
represents. From the absolutely humiliating and underhand assault
and the entirely undignified end he is by a well-understood convention secure. He may lose almost everything but not his heroic
stature. When Antony botches his suicide, mishandling a task
which even his servant discharges effectively, this measure of
protection is withdrawn. He justly compares himself to a tree felled
by an assault its huge strength was never made to withstand:

> and this pine is bark'd
> That overtopp'd them all.

It is the heroic form itself, obsolete under the conditions to which
it is now exposed, and unable to sustain so much as its characteristic
outline, which at the last he knows to be receding into the indistinguishable:

ANTONY. Sometime we see a cloud that's dragonish:
    A vapour sometime like a bear or lion,
    A tower'd citadel, a pendent rock,
    A forked mountain, or blue promontory
    With trees upon't, that nod unto the world,
    And mock our eyes with air: thou hast seen these signs;
    They are black vesper's pageants.
EROS. Ay, my lord.
ANTONY. That which is now a horse, even with a thought
    The rack dislimns, and makes it indistinct
    As water is in water.
EROS. It does, my lord.
ANTONY. My good knave, Eros, now thy captain is
    Even such a body: here I am, Antony,
    Yet cannot hold this visible shape, my knave.

Antony is at the same time a casualty of the great divide between Roman and Egyptian life, which counterpoints the central theme and provides an alternative standard against which it may be judged, or vice versa. The Roman world is typified by the one extended view we are given of it, the long, loveless, oppressive feast on Pompey's galley, which impels even the cipher Lepidus to grope for animation in a dazed way by repeated questions about the 'strange serpents' of Egypt. Roman life is depicted as reaching its apogee in the set occasion, the institution of the banquet, by which the *status quo* celebrates its own rightness and the established order bestows solemn acclaim upon itself. The overwhelming impression is of a closed system from which nothing can ever come but more of the same thing over again. All accounts of orgiastic feasts as a staple part of Egyptian revels come from the mouths of Romans, fastening on the one aspect of delight they understand, appetency tested to destruction point. The glimpses of Egyptian life we get from within are of informal, extra-systematic moments, a night excursion, a fishing expedition, an exchange of banter about sexual fantasies and fecundity between a girl and a soothsayer, evoking the idea of sensuality as a cult, the province of Isis and her mysteries. The Roman outlook is epitomized in the hard, incisive, methodical mind of Octavius himself. With his exact sense of an adversary's weakness, he can not only mock the prodigal enemy but attack the central poetic idea of the play:

> I should have known no less.
> It hath been taught us from the primal state,
> That he which is was wish'd, until he were;
> And the ebb'd man, ne'er lov'd till ne'er worth love,
> Comes dear'd by being lack'd. This common body,
> Like to a vagabond flag upon the stream,
> Goes to and back, lackeying the varying tide,
> To rot itself with motion.

And in the taut intricacy of the thought there is even a mechanical imitation of poetic energy. For it is imperative Octavius should be no shadow opponent, that in seeing the marginal extreme as a graveyard for ineffectives he establishes a truth: the mob and the alcoholic also seek to live without limits, and by no means every attempt to throw off bounds and restraints shows an energetic response. Octavius is not incapable of polishing his image to a cold semblance of magnanimity. Furthermore, he is born to succeed. Yet, even without the commentary of Enobarbus' career as it founders on an understanding of both worlds just sufficient to tear him apart, and his admission in the end that Antony has gone after the more bountiful existence, we are finally left in no difficulty to distinguish the abundance of energy itself from its sad, barren substitute, a life yoked to the idea of dominion, the snare from which, once caught, no man comes smiling.

In his next poetically major play, Shakespeare turned to the ideal which is the antithesis of the ever-varying marginal region explored and realized in *Antony and Cleopatra*. Even if there had been to hand such another piece of near-mythical historiography as Plutarch's story of the downfall of Antonius, it was now inevitable that the great personages of history, the seekers after mastery and office, together with the theme of their crescent and cadent fortunes, should come to be felt as inert and restrictive;[1] and that in any substantial new development they must give way to the kind of character openly alignable with one of the representative figures of traditional myth, or specifically devised to be a vehicle for mythopœic ideas. And in fact, as we shall see, the central figure in *The Winter's Tale* is expressly identified with the most exact counterpart in mythological literature of the royal harlot—Flora, at once goddess and courtesan.[2]

B. *The Winter's Tale*

The Winter's Tale is in one respect without parallel in Shakespeare's work. Nowhere else does he follow one source throughout, but

---

[1] Hence the dearth of poetry in *Coriolanus* that leads Jan Kott aptly to describe it as 'dry as a bone, though violently dramatised', the frenzied impotence of Timon and the exact fittingness of his entombment 'at the very hem of the sea'.

[2] A glance at the goddess's expression in *Primavera* will establish the force of this idea. See also Julius S. Held, 'Flora, Goddess and Courtesan', *Essays in honor of E. Panovsky*, ed. E. Meiss (New York University Press, 1961).

exchange its quite straightforward central motivation for one so improbable that it has exercised his readers ever since. In Greene's *Pandosto*, which was Shakespeare's source, Pandosto [Shakespeare's Leontes] is provoked to jealousy in the most direct way imaginable:

Bellaria [Shakespeare's Hermione], who in her time was the flower of courtesy, willing to shew how unfeignedly she loved her husband by his friend's entertainment, used him likewise so familiarly that her countenance bewrayed how her mind was affected towards him, oftentimes coming herself into his bed chamber to see that nothing should be amiss to mislike him. This honest familiarity increased daily more and more betwixt them; for Bellaria, noting in Egistus [Shakespeare's Polixenes] a princely and bountiful mind, adorned with sundry and excellent qualities, and Egistus, finding in her a virtuous and courteous disposition, there grew such a secret uniting of their affections, that the one could not well be without the company of the other: in so much, that when Pandosto was busied with such urgent affairs that he could not be present with his friend Egistus, Bellaria would walk with him into the garden, where they two in private and pleasant devices would pass away the time to both their contents. This custom still continuing betwixt them, a certain melancholy passion entering the mind of Pandosto drave him into sundry and doubtful thoughts.

Under these circumstances, it would have needed all the explanatory resources of depth psychology if Pandosto had *not* felt angry and jealous. But in *The Winter's Tale* Hermione's conduct is irreproachable, and we need something like Mr. J. I. M. Stewart's persuasive Freudian hypothesis of 'delusional jealousy'[1] to account for Leontes' inexplicable anger and the sudden violence of its onset. It is possible that Shakespeare suddenly became interested in an unusual psychological type, but it seems much more likely that it was necessary for his purpose as a whole to present a mind insulated from all evidence, running on its own involuted circuit which nothing can break.

The unbalanced and incarcerated mind of Leontes is from the first contrasted with the unfailingly stable complex of living forces that he has rejected. Just before he first appears, there is fleetingly

---

[1] *Character and Motive in Shakespeare* (1949), pp. 33 ff.

represented a state of harmony underwritten by the immemorial cycle of nature:

> POLIXENES. Nine changes of the watery star hath been
> The shepherd's note since we have left our throne
> Without a burden.

Before darkness settles, we glimpse an earlier carefree, paradisial way of life, safe under the same unchanging dispensation:

> POLIXENES. We were as twinn'd lambs, that did frisk i' th' sun
> And bleat the one at th' other; what we chang'd
> Was innocence for innocence; we knew not
> The doctrine of ill-doing, nor dream'd
> That any did.

These idyllic images establish for us a sense of the great, permanent, self-regenerating order from which Leontes has isolated himself, but which he cannot destroy. The instability of Leontes' mind and judgement is also brought into contrast with the firmness and trustworthiness of inherited wisdom, as embodied by Apollo's oracle at 'Delphos', whose verdict that Hermione is innocent Leontes defies, and whose traditional sanctities are represented as being in close accord with the abiding certainties of nature:

> CLEOMENES. The climate's delicate, the air most sweet,
> Fertile the isle, the temple much surpassing
> The common praise it bears.
> DION.   I shall report,
> For most it caught me, the celestial habits
> (Methinks I so should term them), and the reverence
> Of the grave wearers. O, the sacrifice,
> How ceremonious, solemn, and unearthly
> It was i' th' offering!

But Leontes' predicament is perhaps realized most pointedly of all in his relationship with the rising generation as personified by Mamillius, his son and heir, who eventually dies on hearing of the injustice done to his mother. The court women spoil the boy, encouraging his prattle because he releases in them a mood of gay coquetry and ministers to their vivacity. His role *vis-à-vis* his father is that of rejuvenator *manqué*. Leontes finds Mamillius day-dreaming and, so far from coming under a loosening or renewing influence, subjects him to a harangue, a tissue of obscure thought and cerebral virtuosity, in the middle of which he suddenly intuits, or so he thinks, that the boy himself has fastened with second sight upon his mother's adultery:

> Come, sir page,
> Look on me with your welkin eye. Sweet villain,
> Most dear'st, my collop! Can thy dam, may't be:
> Affection! Thy intention stabs the centre.
> Thou dost make possible things not so held,
> Communicat'st with dreams—how can this be?
> With what's unreal thou coactive art,
> And fellow'st nothing. Then 'tis very credent
> Thou may'st co-join with something, and thou dost,
> And that beyond commission, and I find it,
> And that to the infection of my brains,
> And hardening of my brows.

Leontes' obsession has formed a mechanical system so closed that it can snatch from deliverance itself confirmation of the worst.

I believe that Shakespeare went out of his way to make the rage of Leontes unjustifiable because he was primarily interested in opposing the icy condition of groundless jealousy and the summer love-idyll so as to set against each other two different processes, the first barren and self-perpetuating, the second fruitful and self-renewing, such an opposition as some illuminated manuscripts of the *Roman de la rose* present so graphically in the contrast between the Castle of Jealousy before and after Venus has surprised it (Pls. 7 *a* and *b*). In its first state the castle is represented as a grim fortress, guarded at every corner by sentries, through whose gateways none come in or go out, and an atmosphere of winter prevails. At the second stage, we are in summer and Venus is in the act of setting fire to the castle. The sentries have disappeared; a throng of men, women, and children, move out of the gateway and across the moat; and on the right a young couple are courting, to the evident disgust of the priest in the procession, who holds up his hands in horror.

Dogs bound happily in all directions. A pair of ducks swim in the moat, and along the castle wall flowers spring up. And it is just such a contrast between the idyllic and the jealous frame of mind as the illuminator realizes here that Shakespeare presents by opposing a pastoral idyll against the jealousy of Leontes. In *The Winter's Tale* the living order is shown to outlast and redeem the mechanical system, but Shakespeare seems to have been more concerned to realize the richness and strength of the one than to explain precisely how in time it supersedes the other. And so I move without more ado to the wonderful pastoral section of the play.

Shakespeare's love idyll, set amidst a sheep-shearing festival, celebrating the sure abundance of nature and the completion of the agricultural cycle, represents our mortal house as consisting of three main storeys. At the simplest, most fundamental level we have the 'twelve Satyrs', impersonated by carters, shepherds, neatherds, and swineherds, who contribute a dance to the festivities. They embody the undiscriminating primary appetites and blind phallic thrust so vividly realized in paintings of them on Greek vases. The middle level, at which the idea of husband is not far distant from that of husbandry, is occupied by the unecstatic and predictable, yet authentic, affairs of the country girls and their lovers:

> CLOWN. If I were not in love with Mopsa, thou shouldst take no
> money of me; but being enthralled as I am, it will also be the
> bondage of certain ribbons and gloves.

But this is an extreme concession by the clown to the demands of courtship, an exceptional departure from his habitual slow deliberation upon sheep and wool:

> Let me see: every 'leven wether tods; every tod yields pound
> and odd shilling; fifteen hundred shorn, what comes the wool
> to? . . . I cannot do't without counters.

It is a relationship holding little or no prospect of rapture, yet one that is ponderably secure. Lastly there is courtly romance, elevated and precarious:

> When you do dance, I wish you
> A wave o' th' sea, that you might ever do
> Nothing but that—move still, still so,
> And own no other function.

Florizel is identifying Perdita, and is rebuked for doing so, with the end of all desire, the moment worthy of permanence which is the object of Faust's quest:

> Werd' ich zum Augenblicke sagen:
> Verweile doch, du bist so schön!
> Dann magst du mich in Fesseln schlagen,
> Dann will ich gern zu Grunde gehn![1]

The whole complex is a sure-founded organic structure of immense resilience at opposite remove from the idea of the ever-fluctuating marginal extreme set forth in *Antony and Cleopatra*; and its seamless unity is further realized in the tendency throughout the play for enrichment in the human sphere to be related to the most rudimentary processes of the life-cycle ('There is some sap in this.' 'Welcome hither, / As is the spring to th' earth'), the sense of what Miss Spurgeon calls 'the oneness of rhythm, the law of movement, in the human emotions with the great fundamental rhythmical movements of nature herself'. The dominant impression made upon us by *The Winter's Tale* as a whole is of this indivisible, firm-rooted, self-re-creating strength.

Yet this massive stability itself presented Shakespeare with a major problem. 'Everything that grows / Holds in perfection but a little moment.' His main difficulty, as for every writer who handles such a theme, was to actualize his idyll, to sustain it as more than an ephemeral instant of equilibrium, whilst staving off the sense of oppressiveness inseparable from the idea of a circumscribed enclave amidst an utterly sure dispensation. This sense of a wearisome sameness Shakespeare seeks to redress in various ways. For instance, just as the idyll is beginning to take shape, he draws on the idea of

---

[1] If I should say to the passing moment, 'Stay, thou art so beautiful', then you may cast me into chains, then I will gladly be annihilated.

the boundless versatility of the gods and invokes the legends of
their metamorphoses, so that we glimpse for a moment a vista in
which all possible developments seem open:

> FLORIZEL.   The gods themselves,
> Humbling their deities to love, have taken
> The shapes of beasts upon them. Jupiter
> Became a bull, and bellow'd; and green Neptune
> A ram, and bleated; and the fire-rob'd god,
> Golden Apollo, a poor humble swain,
> As I seem now.

We shall later find confirmation in *Paradise Lost* that such an idea is
poetically necessary at just this point. But the most effective means
of countering a stultifying sense of repetitiveness and finality was
already present in his source, the idea of the abandoned child who
comes in from the sea:

Let us come to shew the tragical discourse of the young infant.
    Who being tossed with wind and wave floated two whole days
without succour, ready at every puff to be drowned in the sea, till at
last the tempest ceased and the little boat was driven with the tide
into the coast of Sicilia, where sticking upon the sands it rested.
Fortune minding to be wanton, willing to shew that as she hath
wrinkles on her brows so she hath dimples in her cheeks, thought
after so many sour looks to lend a feigned smile, and after a puffing
storm to bring a pretty calm, she began thus to dally.

We have already noticed the intimate association between child
and snake as open and uncommitted structures holding all possibilities intact, definitively expressed in the last scene of *Antony and
Cleopatra*.[1] This fluidity, alarming and even dangerous, is redressed
for ordinary babies by a known parentage and sterilized from the
first by an upbringing in accordance with the traditional *mores* of
their society. With the baby who is exposed and found, these
safeguards are missing and the usually innocent *double-entente*
in 'abandoned' takes on in terms of wantonness a more fateful

---

[1] See p. 53.

significance, a sense of unlimited potentiality. And hence, of course, the formidable innovators and founder-figures represented as having been first let loose on their respective tribes in this way.[1]

In *The Winter's Tale*, the main burden of realizing the idyll's summating level is carried by our abandoned baby, the child whom Leontes, believing it to have been fathered by Polixenes, exposed to the mercy of the waves. It has been found on the shore by the Shepherd, who has carried it home, making the pregnant comment, expressive of the whole atmosphere of the play, 'thou met'st with things dying, I with things new-born'. Now full grown, Perdita, Queen of the feast, her royal origin proclaiming itself even in rural exile, is an intensely attractive figure, partly because of her spontaneity and warm, generous sensuality:

PERDITA.   O, these I lack
  To make you garlands of, and my sweet friend,
  To strew him o'er and o'er!
FLORIZEL.   What, like a corse?
PERDITA. No, like a bank for Love to lie and play on;
  Not like a corse or if, not to be buried,
  But quick and in mine arms.

---

[1] As our argument would lead us to expect, there is overlapping and doubling in this and related connections between child and snake. Apart from the abandoned child *solus* as founder (Moses, Romulus and Remus, etc.), we have Ion, the supposed founder of the Ionic settlements, who was believed to have been abandoned as a child in a cave wearing a necklace of golden snakes. Cecrops, the legendary earth-born founder of Athens, as we noticed earlier, is part snake. As a child, Erectheus, a closely similar Athenian ancestor-figure, was supposedly put in a chest together with two snakes sent by Athena. The insignia of the Duchy of Milan, the first of Alciati's *Emblems*, consist of a snake giving birth to a child. The association between child and snake is further illustrated by the Greek Dioscuri, who in one of their forms were small children and were often represented as snakes (see Nilsson, *M.M.R.*, p. 541). Also by Pausanias' account of the origin of the worship of the hero-god Sosipolis: 'It is said that when the Arcadians had invaded the land of Elis, and the Eleans lay encamped over against them, there came a woman to the captains of the host of the Eleans with a babe at her breast. And she said that the babe was the fruit of her womb, but that she gave him to fight for the Eleans, for so she had been bidden in dreams to do. And the men in authority believed the words of the woman, and they set the child naked in the forefront of the host. So the Arcadians came on, and, lo! the child was changed into a serpent. And fear fell upon the Arcadians at the sight, and they turned to flee, and the Eleans pursued after them, and won a famous victory, and bestowed on the god the name of Sosipolis ("saviour of the city").' (*Description of Greece*, VI. XX. 3.)

Florizel pronounces her 'no shepherdess, but Flora, / Peering in April's front'. Flora's associations are with spring, flowers, and wanton erotic love. Prototype of the flower-girl of popular imagination, she is not among the remote or fearful goddesses; Ovid is particularly insistent[1] that Flora encourages the humble, explaining that prostitutes assist at the Floralia because she likes the common people to support her festival. But Perdita exercises a subtler appeal because, though without Cleopatra's destructiveness, she has a great deal of her imaginative truthfulness and capacity for sudden knowledge. By her exact intuitive feeling for the relation of art to nature she counters and rebuts Polixenes' academic disquisition on this venerable theme. She has a beautifully sharp-edged lucidity of utterance:

> I think affliction may subdue the cheek,
> But not take in the mind.

She scrupulously maintains a distinction between any power she may have in her own right and that associated with her representative role:

>   But that our feasts
> In every mess have folly, and the feeders
> Digest it with a custom, I should blush
> To see you so attir'd; swoon, I think,
> To show myself a glass.

Thus it entirely becomes her to articulate what is poetically the play's decisive moment of truth. She is distributing flowers to old and young, an act whose ritual connotations have so often been remarked on that they need not be emphasized again. Fitting varieties for 'men of middle age' she has in plenty, but such as would be suitable love-tokens for young girls are lacking. There is a powerful sense of midsummer fruition poised to move on into the autumnal, according to its immemorial pattern, with 'the year growing ancient, / Not yet on summer's death nor on the birth / Of

---

[1] 'non est, mihi credite, non est / illa cothurnatas inter habenda deas.' (She is not, believe me she is not, among those superior goddesses.) *Fasti*, v. 347–8.

trembling winter'. Aware of the oppressive near-finality of age and full summer, she suddenly veers towards the idea of the extra-cyclical in lines which evoke it with a sharper poignancy perhaps than any others in our literature:

> O Proserpina,
> For the flowers now, that frighted, thou let'st fall
> From Dis's wagon! Daffodils,
> That come before the swallow dares, and take
> The winds of March with beauty; violets, dim,
> But sweeter than the lids of Juno's eyes
> Or Cytherea's breath; pale primroses,
> That die unmarried ere they can behold
> Bright Phoebus in his strength (a malady
> Most incident to maids); bold oxlips, and
> The crown imperial; lilies of all kinds,
> The flower-de-luce being one.

In Ovid's version of the story, Proserpina is gathering flowers in a grove where spring is eternal. All is perpetually at the beginning: 'perpetuum ver est.'[1] Golding's translation succeeds so poorly in matching the simplicity of Ovid's lines[2] that, in view of the probability that Shakespeare knew the original, a prose rendering is to be preferred:

Not far from Henna's walls there is a deep pool of water, Pergus by name. Not Caÿster on its gliding waters hears more songs of swans than does this pool. A wood crowns the heights around its waters on every side, and with its foliage as with an awning keeps off the sun's hot rays. The branches afford a pleasing coolness, and the well-watered ground bears bright-coloured flowers. There spring is ever-lasting. Within this grove Proserpina was playing, and gathering violets or white lilies. And while with girlish eagerness she was

---

[1] The idea of lasting spring is quite common in relation to earthly paradises, sometimes perhaps meaning no more than that a pleasant season always prevails. In connection with Proserpina, however, it must bear its most exacting sense, as when Dante compares Matelda to Proserpina, 'nel tempo che perdette / la madre lei, ed ella primavera' (When her mother lost her and she forfeited the spring). *Purg.* xxviii. 50–1.

[2] *Metamorphoses*, v. 385–96.

filling her basket and her bosom, and striving to surpass her play-mates in gathering, almost in one act did Pluto see and love and carry her away: so precipitate was his love.

A still more intensely poetic account of the episode opens the beautiful Homeric *Hymn to Demeter*, no text of which was available in Shakespeare's time:

> Separated from Demeter of the golden sword and lovely fruits, she was playing on a soft stretch of grass with the full-breasted daughters of Ocean and gathering flowers—roses, crocuses and violets, irises and hyacinths: and the narcissus which Earth made at the will of Zeus to please the Ever Hospitable as a trap for the girl with face like a budding flower, a marvellous bright flower. It was an awesome thing for deathless gods or mortal men to see: from its root grew a hundred blooms and its smell was very sweet, so that sky and earth and the waves of the sea laughed for joy. And the girl was entranced and reached with both hands for the lovely toy; but the broad-pathed earth opened wide in the plain of Nysa and the Ever Hospitable with his immortal horses, son of Cronos with many names, sprang on her.

There is in the story of Persephone's all too short interlude of play and flower-gathering, as both these poets present it, a most haunt-ing sense of a brief precarious respite of freedom before and outside the inexorable cycle of nature, to which it is decreed later in the story that Persephone must for ever submit herself. If, as we have reason to believe, Persephone was regarded by the Greeks as representing Demeter herself in her youthful aspect, the sense of a primal moment of liberty becomes if anything more acute. By precipitating the essential of this great myth Perdita's lines take on a profoundly anti-pastoral force. Momentarily they enhance the idyll, but at a price, because they make us realize that this cannot be a finally satisfying form. For, although opposed to Leontes' jealousy the pastoral idyll seems wonderfully unconstrained, the idyllic confine cannot maintain its appeal as an image of perfection in company with the idea of liberty, once enjoyed and for ever lost, embodied in the Persephone myth. In seeking to redress the limita-tions of pastoral, Shakespeare discovers the need for its eventual supersession by another kind of ideal, a development with which we shall shortly be concerned.

The other main extra-cyclical element is the one major new character Shakespeare added to Greene's story, Autolycus, the vagabond thief, named after Mercury's son, 'littered' under his planet. Before turning to him, we must pause and consider briefly the extraordinary contrast between the squalor of theft as we see it in the magistrate's court and the august position which the idea of it enjoys in myth and literature. The bird which has made its nest at the top of the tree in our Sumerian myth has to its credit the feat, recounted in the important early Babylonian myth of *Zu*,[1] of stealing the tablets of destiny themselves, so causing cosmic authority to be suspended; Mercury in the evening of his first day alive lifts Apollo's cattle; Prometheus steals fire from Zeus; Ulysses derives resourcefulness from his thieving grandfather Autolycus; and the kingdom of heaven comes 'like a thief in the night'. And here we must digress for a moment, because to understand the importance of Autolycus it is vitally necessary to establish the poetic value of the idea of theft.

Among our own poets, by far the most illuminating on the poetic significance and importance of theft is Wordsworth, for he speaks from immediate knowledge:

> One summer evening (led by her) I found
> A little boat tied to a willow tree
> Within a rocky cave, its usual home.
> Straight I unloosed her chain, and stepping in
> Pushed from the shore. It was an act of stealth
> And troubled pleasure . . .

As all his readers know, this misdemeanour set in motion an episode that initiated a great phase of visionary experience:

> but after I had seen
> That spectacle, for many days, my brain
> Worked with a dim and undetermined sense

[1] *A.N.E.T.*, p. 111.

Of unknown modes of being: o'er my thoughts
There hung a darkness, call it solitude
Or blank desertion. No familiar shapes
Remained, no pleasant images of trees,
Of sea or sky, no colours of green fields;
But huge and mighty forms, that do not live
Like living men, moved slowly through the mind
By day, and were a trouble to my dreams.

Wordsworth's thieving of woodcock precipitated a similar experience:

Sometimes it befel
In these night wanderings, that a strong desire
O'erpowered my better reason, and the bird
Which was the captive of another's toil
Became my prey; and when the deed was done
I heard among the solitary hills
Low breathings coming after me, and sounds
Of undistinguishable motion, steps
Almost as silent as the turf they trod.

Why were theft and numinous experience united for Wordsworth in a single nexus? In speaking of an 'undetermined sense of unknown modes of being' and of 'sounds of undistinguishable motion', he allies these visitations with the profoundly anti-geometrical bias shown throughout the early part of *The Prelude*:

But who shall parcel out
His intellect by geometric rules,
Split like a province into round and square?
Who knows the individual hour in which
His habits were first sown, even as a seed?
Who that shall point as with a wand and say
'This portion of the river of my mind
Came from yon fountain'?

The thief, alert, sudden, a watcher by night (as the Homeric *Hymn to Hermes* stresses), slipping through the set divisions and boundaries on which depends the supremely geometrical institution of property,[1] is in his imaginative aspect a breaker of these anti-poetic, anti-visionary forms. Wordsworth enables us to understand in terms of our own literary experience why it is that the great thieves of myth are felt to be godlike, and why the thief has such an important poetic function to fulfil in relation to idyllic pastoral.

Autolycus, the thief who is our immediate concern, opens the pastoral section of the play by singing a verse about spring exactly in key with Perdita's lines about Proserpina, but strangely counter-seasonal at summer's height:

> When daffodils begin to peer,
> With heigh the doxy over the dale,
> Why, then comes in the sweet o' the year,
> For the red blood reigns in the winter's pale.

He is everywhere the agent of anti-systematic change; he is a pickpocket, a 'snapper-up of unconsidered trifles'; it is he who enables Florizel to escape aboard ship by exchanging clothes with him; the divide between court and country and that between master and servant present no obstacle to him, and he is able to fleece the shepherd by posing in his borrowed finery as a person of eminence about the king's business. But the point of all these activities is most sharply and poetically realized when the country girls clamour for a ballad and he articulates for them in a song about a mysterious journey their acute longing that the foreseeably uneventful progression of their days may somehow break into the unknown:

AUTOLYCUS. Get you hence, for I must go
   Where it fits not you to know.
DORCUS. Whither?
MOPSA. O whither?
DORCUS. Whither?

---

[1] One small but extremely significant deviation from his source suggests that the idea of transgressing these very divisions was critically important to Shakespeare in relation to idyllic pastoral. In *Pandosto*, Dorastus (Florizel) encounters Fawnia (Perdita) at a meeting of all the farmers' daughters in Sicily on his way home from a hawking expedition. Shakespeare, seizing on the hawk's disdain of boundaries, makes the bird itself the cause of a quite different first meeting:
  FLORIZEL.   I bless the time
  When my good falcon made her flight across
  Thy father's ground.

MOPSA. It becomes thy oath full well,
   Thou to me thy secrets tell.
DORCUS. Me too: let me go thither.
MOPSA. Or thou goest to th' grange or mill.
DORCUS. If to either, thou dost ill.
AUTOLYCUS. Neither.
DORCUS. What, neither?
AUTOLYCUS. Neither.
DORCUS. Thou hast sworn my love to be.
MOPSA. Thou hast sworn it more to me.
   Then whither goest? Say whither?

And this is momentarily to elude the oppression of a cyclical mode of life, of an inexorable archetypal pattern that has obtained from the beginning. It is, in a quite unphilosophical sense, to point to the Beyond.

But, as we have said, it is the overwhelming sense in *The Winter's Tale* of an immemorial and repetitive continuity, no less than the circumscribed nature of the idyllic confine, that calls forth and makes poetically necessary these compensating extra-cyclical elements. The final act moves towards the presentation of a reunified society, once more assured of a future. The home-coming of the young lovers restores to an entire community man's ancient hope that his children may possess the land of their forefathers, or as Leontes expresses it, before they have been identified, in patriarchal language:

> O, alas!
> I lost a couple, that 'twixt heaven and earth
> Might thus have stood, begetting wonder, as
> You, gracious couple, do;

Now the sense of the distant past, the imaginative life of many generations, which was hinted at earlier by the description of the oracle and by Mamillius' comment, 'a sad tale's best for Winter', and which is implicit in the title of the play, becomes more emphatic.

This news, which is called true, is so like an old tale that the verity of it is in strong suspicion.

Like an old tale still, which will have matter to rehearse, though
credit be asleep, and not an ear open . . .

> That she is living,
> Were it but told you, should be hooted at
> Like an old tale.

Whereas in *Antony and Cleopatra* it is sudden knowledge that
predominates, in *The Winter's Tale* the emphasis is upon inherited
wisdom and lore, knowledge that hath been ever of old. At this
stage of the play, the 'grave and good' Paulina, who has tenaciously
watched over Hermione for sixteen years, and embodies all that is
best and strongest in traditional morality, faithful as the turtle-
dove, symbol of constancy, to which she compares herself, enters
into her own and organizes the unfolding of events. The disclosure
of the living Hermione is enacted in a chapel, a building whose
atmosphere is determined by those rites through which we commit
our dead to the timeless, yet keep them folded within a human and
institutional continuity, a shrine largely given over to that ancestral
world which persistently asserts itself in *The Winter's Tale*:

> O sir!
> You have undone a man of fourscore three,
> That thought to fill his grave in quiet; yea,
> To die upon the bed my father died,
> To lie close by his honest bones . . .

After Hermione has at last revealed herself,[1] Leontes' response,
once he has recovered from his amazement that she is alive, is
restrained, even muted. The older generation can now look for a
personal consummation only in healing the wounds of the past to
which they belong, whereas the great deliverance is a supra-personal
one, reprieve from what Leontes has acknowledged his supreme
punishment, to be left without issue. Nevertheless, there is a place

---

[1] It would fall in with my argument to assign considerable poetic importance—
living form superseding inorganic form—to the statue-episode which is the climax of
the action, but I cannot do so with conviction, not being among those who find it
entirely satisfying. An element of contrived allegory in the basic idea seems to me to
be reflected in a degree of staginess and its only half-successful transmutation into
dramatic poetry.

for the remainder of their lives, a social order capable of harbouring them, for this is not the world of *Antony and Cleopatra*, which has no room for age, nor indeed a single aged character.

To think of *The Winter's Tale* is to become aware of our deep desire to perpetuate the inherited order, of its miraculous power to re-create itself, of our absolute need for the certain domicile that it affords. It is to realize the oneness of human life with the natural cycle of which it is a part and the bond uniting even ideal manifestations of that life with the fundamental drives which man shares with the rest of nature. And the final impression which the play leaves in our minds is of this enduring integrity. Dr. Leavis speaks with penetrating exactness of the effect which *The Winter's Tale* has upon us 'as of the sap rising from the root'.[1] The extra-cyclical, which I have stressed because it is of deep consequence, and the work's most neglected aspect, is a recessive element. Essentially, *The Winter's Tale* is a great many-tiered image of self-renewing organic strength and sure fulfilment, crowned with the delicate flower of high romance, embracing those less ambitious, steadfast affections which are the guarantee of social continuity, grounded in the rhythms of agriculture and the chthonic roots of life itself. It exhibits with severe exactness the characteristics we ascribed at the outset in rough and approximate terms to the tree, combining all those aspects in which, as the Old Testament[2] puts it, 'the tree is the life of man'.[3]

Our existence would be immeasurably simpler if Cleopatra's world in *Antony and Cleopatra* or that of *The Winter's Tale* alone presented itself to us as ideal, if either of them were entirely satisfying, or if we could think of both as being combined in some arcadia or idyllic confine. In all too evident fact, however, we require both of these dimensions and cannot conceive of an earthly paradise that would unite them. And so there remained a final task: to unify the opposite poetic themes which had severally prevailed in the one play and in the other by realizing and defining their origin and

---

[1] *The Common Pursuit* (1952), p. 181.   [2] Deut. 20: 19.
[3] For an account of the importance of the tree as a specific motif in Renaissance thought, and an extensive bibliography, see G. B. Ladner, 'Vegetation Symbolism and the Concept of Renaissance', *Essays in Honour of E. Panovsky*, ed. Meiss (1961).

terminus in imaginative activity itself. For snake-like and tree-like structures, reflecting the long human endeavour at once to frequent the ever-varying marginal extreme and possess the sure habitation of an enduring order, make their profound appeal to imagination in the last analysis by reason of their correspondence with its own inner processes; because to reconcile the contrary ideals which these images express, together with their related modes of thought and feeling, a labour imposed upon man by his imagination, is the most distinctive function of that selfsame faculty; and, in the body of myth we began by considering, the snake is the *guardian* of the tree, and both are folded in a single image. Shakespeare now broke with traditional forms of thought and turned to material distinguished by the rarest characteristic in literature or art: that the figures whose mythopœic force is most palpable are yet to a great extent constructions of the individual mind.

C. *The Tempest*

Long before he wrote *The Tempest*, Shakespeare had given in a famous passage near the end of *A Midsummer Night's Dream* the most poetic and exact general definition of imagination ever set down:

> The poet's eye, in a fine frenzy rolling,
> Doth glance from heaven to earth, from earth to heaven;
> And, as imagination bodies forth
> The forms of things unknown, the poet's pen
> Turns them to shapes, and gives to airy nothing
> A local habitation and a name.[1]

His ultimate achievement was to provide concrete embodiment for that very form-giving capability itself. The central theme of *The Tempest* is not ideal pleasure but the nature and essential structure of imaginative power.

In barest outline, *The Tempest* tells the story of an exiled duke who for a limited time exercises prodigious power on an island, subjugating and enslaving two native creatures of the region through the

[1] V. i. 12–17.

art of formulation as represented by his books and spells, a servitude from which they both incessantly seek to liberate themselves. He controls them for a period with authority, qualified by a deep uneasiness, and then, forswearing magic, sets them free and reassumes ordinary mortal concerns. The love story and the political conspiracy are subordinate, aside from the main current of poetic vitality. Because of its substantial breach with inherited forms[1] and its combination of high seriousness with child-like elements, *The Tempest* requires of us sudden transitions from the sophisticated to the naïve response; and we can only hope to understand Prospero's two strange minions, and his crucially important relationship with them, by patiently observing their actual characteristics with as few preconceptions as possible, and by refraining from any attempt to force them into an abstract scheme or rehabilitate them in a more technical idiom.

Caliban, the dispossessed lord of the island, is inhumanizable and ineducable, a creature 'on whose nature / Nurture can never stick'. No rationally devised discipline will make him better, and he enjoys a natural immunity from improvers of all kinds, be they magicians, pedagogues, or divines; for he is a 'monster', equipped with the defence-mechanism of an indomitable shapelessness. But such educators can disturb the harmony he once enjoyed at a lower level of complexity, and this is what Prospero has done:

> You taught me language and my profit on't
> Is, I know how to curse: the red plague rid you
> For learning me your language.

The plagues he invokes (toads, beetles, bats, fogs, the air of fens) affiliate him with the ditch-world of Poor Tom in *King Lear*, who

eats the swimming frog, the toad, the tadpole, the wall-newt and the water; that in the fury of his heart, when the foul fiend rages, eats cow-dung for sallets; swallows the old rat and the ditch-dog; drinks the green mantle of the standing pool.

He is murderous; he has no concept of sexual restraint; he is fickle

---

[1] For the case against treating analogues and pseudo-sources as of any importance for this play, see Kermode's Introduction to the Arden Edition, p. lxx.

and in the short-term subservient to any master who can frighten
him or further his ends. Yet he is intimately acquainted with the
difference between fruitful and barren ground and able to guide his
human masters to the fertile places:

> and then I lov'd thee
> And show'd thee all the qualities o' th' isle,
> The fresh springs, brine-pits, barren place, and fertile.

If we took notice of the sense of the words alone, George Herbert
might without incongruity have written of him, and not the
Creator,

> He leads me to the tender grass,
> Where I both feed and rest;
> Then to the streams that gently pass:
> In both I have the best.

And it accords with this function that he should be delicately
attuned to the creatures of the earth:[1]

> Pray you, tread softly, that the blind mole may not
> Hear a foot fall . . .

The mysterious elements of the island are not alien to his mind, nor
do they frighten him:

> Be not afeared: the isle is full of noises,
> Sounds and sweet airs, that give delight, and hurt not.
> Sometimes a thousand twangling instruments
> Will hum about mine ears; and sometimes voices,
> That, if I then had wak'd after long sleep,
> Will make me sleep again: and then, in dreaming,
> The clouds methought would open and show riches
> Ready to drop upon me; that, when I wak'd
> I cried to dream again.

[1] Cf. the description in the *Epic of Gilgamesh* of Gilgamesh's half-human *alter ego*
Enkidu (Ambassador to the underworld in our Sumerian myth):
His body was covered with matted hair like Samuqan's, the god of cattle. He was
innocent of mankind; he knew nothing of the cultivated land. Enkidu ate grass in the
hills with the gazelle and jostled with wild beasts at the water-holes; he had joy of
the water with the herds of wild game. *E.G.*, p. 61.

He responds to the experience and desires to extend it, as if it aroused some haunting dream of a richer life. And he is able to recognize with intuitive exactness that Prospero's inherited formulative resources are the one thing he must fear:

> Remember
> First to possess his books, for without them
> He's but a sot, as I am, nor hath not
> One spirit to command: they all do hate him
> As rootedly as I. Burn but his books.

Even his licentiousness is totally distinct from blind appetite, and his reproductive instincts are directed by a sure sense of what is, and is not, worth producing over again:

> And that most deeply to consider is
> The beauty of his daughter; he himself
> Calls her a nonpareil: I never saw a woman,
> But only Sycorax my dam and she;
> But she as far surpasseth Sycorax
> As great'st does least.

Being avid for anything that offers the prospect of freedom, he is easily gulled and humiliated by the degenerate Stephano and Trinculo, and yet they cannot debase him as they do themselves, because he reacts to the 'celestial liquor' simply as something that widens his horizons and presages liberty:

> 'Ban, 'Ban, Ca–Caliban
> Has a new master—Get a new man.

> Freedom, high-day! high-day, freedom! freedom! high-day, freedom!

Furthermore, in the long run he is not mocked or deceived by bids to control him through the counterfeit semblance of power:

> What a thrice-double ass
> Was I, to take this drunkard for a god,
> And worship this dull fool!

Prospero's relationship with Caliban is one of censorious dependence. He cannot disown him or afford to get rid of him, and the only penalties he inflicts are puerile injuries in the literal sense, pinches, pricking by hedgehogs, the embraces of snakes, and other inconveniences such as small children would administer with keen delight:

> His spirits hear me,
> And yet I needs must curse. But they'll nor pinch,
> Fright me with urchin-shows, pitch me i' the mire,
> Nor lead me, like a firebrand, in the dark,
> Out of my way, unless he bid 'em: but
> For every trifle are they set upon me:
> Sometimes like apes, that mew and chatter at me
> And after bite me; then like hedgehogs, which
> Lie tumbling in my bare-foot way and mount
> Their pricks at my foot-fall: sometime am I
> All wound with adders, who with cloven tongues
> Do hiss me into madness.

Prospero may command and denounce, but his only direct and palpable contact with Caliban is through these torments executed for him by Ariel, and the childlike immediacy they exhibit. This idea of childlike hurtfulness is strangely persistent in *The Tempest* and is taken up again later in the play when Caliban and his confederates are driven through 'toothed briers, sharp furzes, pricking goss and thorns' and 'pinch-spotted by goblins'. In his relations with Caliban, Prospero shows much of the *naïveté* and directness we find in children, not as it often suits us to idealize them, but as they really are.

Ariel's prime characteristic, on the other hand, is his unlimited formal diversity, adaptable to every element except the earth:

> All hail, great master! grave sir, hail! I come
> To answer thy best pleasure; be't to fly,
> To swim, to dive into the fire, to ride
> On the curl'd clouds: to thy strong bidding task
> Ariel and all his quality.

He is unimaginably swift and heir to Puck, who could 'put a girdle round about the earth / In forty minutes':

> I drink the air before me, and return
> Or e'er your pulse twice beat.

It is the same idea of speed that seizes Dante's imagination as he and
Beatrice enter the Heaven of Mercury:

> And as the mark is by the arrow smit
> before the cord forgets to quiver, thus
> into the Second Kingdom did we flit.[1]

The most important clues to Ariel's essential nature are provided
by the specific forms he assumes in his sudden metamorphoses. His
first transformation is to make himself 'like a nymph of the sea'.
Sea-nymphs are in essence Nature's borderers, frequenting the
margin between the formed and the formless, and that alien and
unsure extreme is for them a natural habitat. To this verge between
sea and land, where the most fateful, though invisible, transactions
in *The Tempest* take place, Ariel beckons Ferdinand:

> Come unto these yellow sands,
>   And then take hands:
> Curtsied when you have, and kiss'd,—
>   The wild waves whist,—
> Foot it featly here and there;
> And, sweet sprites, the burden bear.
>   Hark, hark!
>   [*Burden*: Bow, wow, *dispersedly.*]
>   The watch-dogs bark:
>   [*Burden*: Bow, wow, *dispersedly.*]
>   Hark, hark! I hear
> The strain of strutting Chanticleer
>   Cry, Cock-a-diddle-dow.

This is a region whose other natural occupants, together with
children, are dogs, both by imaginative congruity in virtue of their
alert wantonness and in literal fact, as observation on the beach will

---

[1]   E sì come saetta, che nel segno
      percote pria che sia la corda queta,
      così corremmo nel secondo regno.

                              (*Paradiso*, v. 91–3)

confirm,[1] and it has strong associations with the ideas suggested by dawn's first cockcrow, the openness and limitless promise of daybreak. The sounds of dogs making up the refrain and the concluding cry of the cock are in no way comic or extraneous. And Ariel transforms himself into a creature of this marginal region, just as he invites the young prince to set foot within it, essentially because it is his own true milieu.

Ariel later transforms himself into a harpy so as to disrupt the conspirators' banquet:

Thunder and lightning. Enter ARIEL *like a harpy: claps his wings upon the table; and, with a quaint device, the banquet vanishes.*

And Prospero specially praises his performance in this role:

> Bravely the figure of this harpy hast thou
> Perform'd, my Ariel; a grace it had, devouring:
> Of my instruction hast thou nothing bated
> In what thou hadst to say. . . .

It is necessary at this point to seek some understanding of harpies. They are first described in Hesiod's *Theogony* as beautiful creatures of the wind:

Thaumas married Electra, the daughter of the deep Ocean-stream: she gave birth to flying Iris and to the Harpies, Aëllo and Ocypetes, whose streaming hair is so beautiful, and who, as they soar above on their speedy wings, are as fast as birds or gusts of wind.[2]

They have this same grace in the representations on the fifth-century Harpy Tomb from Xanthus in the British Museum; but later they degenerate into foul predators, whose main role from the *Argonautica* onwards is to break up feasts by snatching the food, mysteriously emerging from loathsomeness during the Renaissance period to take on an association with abundance.[3] Classical scholars have been

---

[1] Compare also the dogs playing on the shore in Piero di Cosimo's *Mythological Scene*, National Gallery.

[2] *Theogony*, 265 ff.

[3] See, for instance, Dürer's *Harpies with Cornucopias* (Kestner Museum, Hanover), and the harpies on the corners of the altar in Raphael's *The Sacrifice at Lystra* (Victoria and Albert Museum, London).

puzzled by them and some have attributed the earlier change, a little bashfully, to the Ancients having heard rumours of a certain species of Indian fruit-eating bat.[1] I think there is a more plausible explanation, to be taken together with the snatching propensity indicated by their name. A banquet, as we have said, celebrates the rightness of the *status quo*, and there is ample testimony to the lurking fear of intervention by anything opposed to the precarious equilibrium of an occasion of this kind. It is just as the feast has been set that the Ancient Mariner clutches the Wedding Guest; and Erasmus records in his *Adagia* that in old times, whenever silence fell in the middle of a feast, it was believed that Mercury was passing, adding that in his own day such a silence was felt to be ominous.[2] The felt hostility of the limitlessly various and elusive—whether it be a wind spirit, Ariel, or Mercury—to the rites by which we seek to solemnize the established order, and its consequent potential for arousing fear and revulsion, are surely plain enough to save us from resorting to the Indian bats. The harpies, I suggest, became disrupters of feasts mainly because they were felt to represent a principle in man which is opposed to those elements within him that are expressed in the ritual of the banquet. Thus, in taking upon himself the role of harpy, Ariel reveals himself as embodying this anti-festive principle.

Boundlessly versatile, a creature of the marginal extreme, at enmity with set occasions and static forms, Ariel inevitably seeks to be released from Prospero's tyranny, and he clamours ever more insistently for his freedom:

> Is there more toil? Since thou dost give me pains,
> Let me remember thee what thou hast promis'd
> Which is not yet perform'd me.

PROSPERO.   How now! moody?
What is't thou canst demand?

ARIEL.   My liberty.

He cannot be content until he discharges no services and can sever all commitment to form itself as an intolerable restriction. His

---

[1] See *Oxford Classical Dictionary*, p. 405.
[2] *Adagia*, IV. IV. xci.

principle of life is to be perpetually at the beginning, where every possibility of development is intact. The opening of Autolycus' lyric, 'When daffodils begin to peer', foreshadows Ariel, and, when he finally receives his liberty, its image derives from the natural cycle at precisely its first barely discernible hint of commitment to a form:

> Merrily, merrily shall I live now
> Under the blossom that hangs on the bough.

The most poignant lines in the play come when we learn that the vestigial common bond of sharing for a time with man a physical outline seems to have instilled in Ariel a glimmer of kindness:

ARIEL. . . . your charm so strongly works them,
　　That if you now beheld them, your affections
　　Would become tender.
PROSPERO. 　　　　　Dost thou think so, spirit?
ARIEL. Mine would, sir, were I human.
PROSPERO. 　　　　　　　　And mine shall.
　　Hast thou, which art but air, a touch, a feeling
　　Of their afflictions, and shall not myself,
　　One of their kind, that relish all as sharply,
　　Passion as they, be kindlier mov'd than thou art?

Prospero has released Ariel from a pine tree, where the witch Sycorax had confined him:

> And, for thou wast a spirit too delicate
> To act her earthy and abhorr'd commands,
> Refusing her grand hests, she did confine thee,
> By help of her more potent ministers,
> And in her most unmitigable rage,
> Into a cloven pine; within which rift
> Imprison'd, thou didst painfully remain
> A dozen years; within which space she died
> And left thee there, where thou didst vent thy groans
> As fast as mill-wheels strike.

And to such another penitentiary, the ultimate deterrent, our argument suggests, for one whose native region is the marginal extreme, Prospero threatens to return Ariel, if he is not submissive:

> If thou more murmur'st, I will rend an oak
> And peg thee in his knotty entrails till
> Thou hast howl'd away twelve winters.

But he also plies Ariel with anxious endearments ('That's my delicate Ariel', etc.), such as might be addressed to a fickle but favoured son, or some irreplaceable foreign domestic on a nebulous contract.

The central theme of *The Tempest* hinges upon Prospero's ambivalent relationship with his two servants, his dependence for supreme control upon creatures who fulfil in relation to it a double role as preservers and destroyers, and whose common principle of life is to liberate themselves from the tyranny they support, an apparent contradiction set forth with precision beyond the reach of abstract thought, by the ancient image of the snake-encircled tree. *The Tempest* approaches anew the heart of the tree–snake configuration, the unitive principle without which it could not work upon us as one entire image but would only express incompatible objectives and unharmonizable ends, an achievement to be carefully distinguished from the mere coupling of fresh variants of its component motifs. Or to put it another way, the play sets forth that function of the mind which reconciles the contrary elements within itself which tree and snake present to us. *This unitive principle is now defined not in terms of an opposition between particular symbolic figures but through the structure of Prospero's power, his establishment of organization through complicity with the subversive, the collaboration between his inherited knowledge and beings at enmity with it, and the upholding of his charm by the very forces which require that it shall dissolve.* For it is the central paradox of imaginative activity that not only are the forms by which it bodies forth the unknown swept into obsolescence, even as they come into being, by form-resistant and anarchic forces, so that as one of the foremost poets of our generation has put it, 'one has only learnt to get the better of words / For the thing one no longer has to say, or the way in which / One is no longer disposed to say it', but that these essentially seditious forces are themselves, no less than his inherited wisdom and understanding, a vital source of the form-giver's mastery and integrative strength. Were it not so, his task would be hopeless as well as fearful. It is the cardinal fact of the imaginative life, and one which we have to learn by experience, indeed over and over again. And this process can only be realized in its own poetic or symbolic terms because, like the elements in the mind which it unites, it has no true equivalent in abstract discourse.

The broad interpretation of *The Tempest* I am putting forward having been indicated, we must now revert to its concrete detail. Caliban and Ariel, as we have just said, are both preservers and destroyers of Prospero's mastery. Their constructive role is to mediate between their overlord and his island, for even though ever striving to free themselves from Prospero's tyranny, they put at his disposal the interior lines of communication which they enjoy in their different ways within his domain, whose subtleties manifest to us the true nature and reach of his power more forcibly than any of his obvious exhibitions of magical control. Its atmosphere and character are intensively established in the lines immediately following Ariel's song 'Come unto these yellow sands':

FERDINAND. Where should this music be? i' th' air, or th' earth?
It sounds no more;—and sure, it waits upon
Some god o' th' island. Sitting on a bank,
Weeping again the king my father's wrack,
This music crept by me upon the waters,
Allaying both their fury, and my passion,
With its sweet air: thence I have follow'd it,—
Or it hath drawn me rather,—but 'tis gone.
No, it begins again.

[ARIEL *sings*]
Full fathom five thy father lies;
Of his bones are coral made:
Those are pearls that were his eyes:
Nothing of him that doth fade,
But doth suffer a sea-change
Into something rich and strange.

Sea-nymphs hourly ring his knell:
                    [*Burden*: ding-dong.]
            Hark! now I hear them,—ding-dong, bell.
FERDINAND. The ditty does remember my drown'd father.
        This is no mortal business, nor no sound
        That the earth owes. . . .

Whatever is said about this poetry must seem either too little or too much, and it is in the first of these directions that I hope to err. For many of us, assisted perhaps by *The Waste Land*, the entire effect of *The Tempest* in retrospection is summed up in the words,

                Sitting on a bank,
        Weeping again the king my father's wrack,
        This music crept by me upon the waters,
        Allaying both their fury, and my passion
        With its sweet air:

The young prince sitting on the bank, his tears over his father's wreck, the tangential movement of the music on the water: these images present with strange potency a reconciliation of the inherited order with the marginal and the extra-systematic. Throughout the whole passage there persists the image of music. And music is of all purposeful forms we have devised the most elusive to the senses, the least amenable to geometry, an incorrigible trespasser infiltrating past all the barriers, mental as well as physical, which we may have established, and as such has been immemorially valued and feared as a medium by which for good or ill the strongly established may be changed; and these associations are enhanced here by the music's indefinite source and capricious intermittence. In *Antony and Cleopatra*, it will be remembered, just such unlocatable music presages the dissolution of the heroic form that is Antony. The wonderful song 'Full Fathom Five' has a related theme, metamorphosis by water, a transmutation of the drowned father and the inherited structure he stands for within the unfathomed and formless element. Its underlying conception is strongly allied to the New Testament saying, 'Except a man be born again of water and the spirit he cannot enter the kingdom of heaven', as also to the Babylonian cosmogonist's belief that Ocean is the primordial creative source; and its basic symbolism of death and renewal by immersion is enshrined in the Order of Baptism, not on the whole associated for us with the rich and strange, both in the rite itself and in the prayer that the regenerated infant 'may crucify the old man'. But the idea is one we may best come to understand not by tracing all its various historical and anthropological manifestations but by attending to such poetry in *The Tempest* itself as that we have just been considering. At the centre of Prospero's power lies his command of the process which this poetry expresses, for the lord of the island is master also through his intermediaries of the forces which operate in and around it.

Just before the end of Act Three, when Prospero's ascendancy is at its height, and has just been associated in visual terms with his command of form by the re-entry and dance of 'the Shapes', comes the play's turning-point, the first definite hint that his magic is subject to a lease which is almost due to expire:

> My high charms work,
> And these mine enemies are all knit up
> In their distractions. . . .

We need not make such claims about what quite securely and indubitably works. An eventual abdication was inevitable, given Prospero's dependence for mastery upon servants whose overriding aim is to rid themselves of it and be free. From now on, emphasis shifts away from the exercise of collected power towards its impending dispersal, and this transition, its one truly dramatic element, dominates the play. A few lines later, Alonso foreshadows the destined end when he dimly recognizes for the first time the true origin of power:

> and the thunder,
> That deep and dreadful organ-pipe, pronounc'd
> The name of Prosper: it did bass my trespass.
> Therefore my son i' th' ooze is bedded; and
> I'll seek him deeper than e'er plummet sounded,
> And with him there lie mudded.

Henceforward Prospero fixes upon Ariel a troubled concentration
felt in his next conciliatory greeting:

> What, Ariel! my industrious servant Ariel!

Ariel's immediate task is to present the Masque, a spectacle Prospero
marshals with a curious detachment which he does not conceal:

> I must
> Bestow upon the eyes of this young couple
> Some vanity of mine art: it is my promise,
> And they expect it from me.

The Goddesses Iris, Ceres, and Juno now present themselves to the
accompaniment of soft music. The task of Ceres and Juno is to
confer upon the lovers the blessing of sure continuance, the bene-
diction of *The Winter's Tale*:

> JUNO. Honour, riches, marriage-blessing,
> Long continuance, and increasing,
> Hourly joys be still upon you!
> Juno sings her blessings on you.
> CERES. Earth's increase, foison plenty,
> Barns and garners never empty;
> Vines, with clustering bunches growing;
> Plants with goodly burden bowing;
> Spring come to you at the farthest
> In the very end of harvest!
> Scarcity and want shall shun you;
> Ceres' blessing so is on you.

The role of Iris, the rainbow-goddess, on the other hand, is to
invoke and secure the favour of the creatures of the marginal region,
the province of Cleopatra:

> IRIS. You nymphs, call'd Naiades, of the windring brooks,
> With your sedg'd crowns, and ever-harmless looks,
> Leave your crisp channels, and on this green land
> Answer your summons; Juno does command.
> Come, temperate nymphs, and help to celebrate
> A contract of true love; be not too late.[1]

[1] This interpretation is not intended to exclude the connection of nymphs with
chastity, but plainly in the lines spoken by Iris the phrases which convey their
marginal associations are poetically the stronger.

The harmonious conjunction of the continuing and the ever-varying is next realized in visual terms by the joining together of Reapers and Nymphs 'in a graceful dance'. Ferdinand, entranced by the pageant, is innocent enough to suppose that the momentary vision can be translated into a permanent material order, an earthly Elysium:

FERDINAND.   Let me live here ever;
            So rare a wonder'd father and a wise,
            Makes this place Paradise.

But Prospero knows only too well that these apparitions are but secondary manifestations, enactments of his fancy, as he calls them, and that this fleeting *rapprochement* with pastoral, even though figuring forth its basic structure, is a distraction from his main concern. Towards the end of the dance of the Reapers and Nymphs, he 'starts suddenly, and speaks; after which, to a strange hollow, and confused noise, they heavily vanish', for he has recalled the imminent attack of Caliban and his confederates:

            I had forgot that foul conspiracy
            Of the beast Caliban, and his confederates
            Against my life: the minute of their plot
            Is almost come.—[*to the* SPIRITS] Well done;—
            Avoid! No more!

It is as if this traffic in inferior forms and pandering to naïve expectations might have proved the undoing of his whole project.

In the speech by Prospero which follows, Shakespeare consummates all that he had hinted at and prefigured when Antony described himself as becoming 'indistinguishable as water is in water'. He proclaims the assignment with dissolution of vast inherited forms, the great monuments set up to proclaim dynastic power and withstand change, and with them of the most substantial inheritance of all, the world itself:

            Our revels now are ended. These our actors,
            As I foretold you, were all spirits and
            Are melted into air, into thin air:

> And, like the baseless fabric of this vision,
> The cloud-capp'd towers, the gorgeous palaces,
> The solemn temples, the great globe itself,
> Yea, all which it inherit, shall dissolve
> And, like this insubstantial pageant faded,
> Leave not a rack behind. We are such stuff
> As dreams are made on; and our little life
> Is rounded with a sleep.

'All which it inherit, shall dissolve.' But in the image of the 'cloud-capp'd towers' the idea of the permanent structure merges with that of the dissolving form, so that the one seems to have been built out of the other. And the great inheritance, like the pageant, has been run up out of the insubstantial, to which it must return. Finally, having realized in poetic terms that union of the enduring with the limitlessly various by which man may after a fashion bind and enclose the Infinite, Shakespeare gently and severely draws around life itself the one boundless encompassment imagination can accept.

The assassination bid is crushed, and punishment meted out of a kind we are by now familiar with, pursuit by Spirits in the shape of dogs. The sense of borrowed time, an all but usurped limit, is now acute:

> Now does my project gather to a head,
> My charms crack not, my spirits obey. . . .

Ariel makes his plea for tenderness towards the conspirators and is sent to release them. Then Prospero acknowledges that his ascendancy has depended upon creatures of the marginal region, no less than upon the inherited wisdom represented by his book, abjures his art, and proclaims his impending resignation of all super-human power:

> Ye elves of hills, brooks, standing lakes, and groves;
> And ye, that on the sands with printless foot
> Do chase the ebbing Neptune and do fly him
> When he comes back; you demi-puppets, that
> By moonshine do the green sour ringlets make
> Whereof the ewe not bites; and you, whose pastime

Is to make midnight mushrumps; that rejoice
To hear the solemn curfew; by whose aid,—
Weak masters though ye be—I have bedimm'd
The noontide sun, call'd forth the mutinous winds,
And 'twixt the green sea and the azur'd vault
Set roaring war: to the dread-rattling thunder
Have I given fire and rifted Jove's stout oak
With his own bolt: the strong bas'd promontory
Have I made shake; and by the spurs pluck'd up
The pine and cedar: graves at my command
Have wak'd their sleepers, op'd, and let them forth
By my so potent art. But this rough magic
I here abjure; and, when I have requir'd
Some heavenly music,—which even now I do,—
To work mine end upon their senses that
This airy charm is for, I'll break my staff,
Bury it certain fathoms in the earth,
And deeper than did ever plummet sound,
I'll drown my book.

The opening lines of the speech recall those earlier borderers of
A Midsummer Night's Dream:

And never, since the middle summer's spring,
Met we on hill, in dale, forest, or mead,
By paved fountain, or by rushy brook,
Or in the beached margent of the sea,
To dance our ringlets to the whistling wind,
But with thy brawls thou has disturb'd our sport.

Its first part is substantially borrowed from a passage[1] in Ovid's
version of the story of Jason and Medea, apparently from the
original in conjunction with Golding's translation:

Ye airs and winds, ye elves of hills, of brooks, of woods alone,
Of standing lakes, and of the night approach ye everychone.
Through help of whom (the crooked banks much wond'ring at the
    thing)
I have compelled streams to run clean backward to their spring.

[1] *Metamorphoses*, vii. 198–206.

By charms I make the calm seas rough, and make the rough seas
    plain
And cover all the sky with clouds, and chase them thence again.
By charms I raise and lay the winds, and burst the viper's jaw,
And from the bowels of the earth both stones and trees do draw.
Whole woods and forests I remove; I make the mountains shake,
And even the earth itself to groan and fearfully to quake.
I call up dead men from their graves; and thee O lightsome Moon
I darken oft, though beaten brass abate thy peril soon.
Our sorcery dims the morning fair, and darks the sun at noon.
The flaming breath of firie bulls ye quenched for my sake
And caused their unwieldy necks the bended yoke to take.
Among the earthbred brothers you a mortal war did set
And brought asleep the dragon fell whose eyes were never shet.

Jason and Medea have just returned to Thessaly with the Golden
Fleece, and Medea is invoking the aid of various divinities in finding a magic juice which may restore the health and strength of
youth to the dying father of Jason. The unsleeping serpent of the
last line is, of course, the protector of the tree on which hangs the
Fleece, 'the awful guardian of the golden tree' as Ovid describes
him.[1] Our interpretation of *The Tempest* would lead us to expect
Shakespeare to be strongly attracted at this climactic moment by a
story with a snake-encircled tree as its central image, and just such
a legend, as we see here, is the one source which we can be absolutely
certain that he in fact recollected and actually used in writing
The Tempest. And it seems to me overwhelmingly probable that
Shakespeare found himself drawn to this source mainly because its
imaginative centre coincided with that of his own play. In the
final section from 'But this rough magic' onwards, which is all
Shakespeare's own, Prospero declares that he will give back the
apparatus of his power to the elements from which they had their
origin, his wooden staff to the earth, and the more potent tool, his
book, to the great waters. Perhaps the simplest way of emphasizing
the exact rightness of this climax is to turn to a well-remembered
figure who dispossessed himself in an almost identical way:

[1] *Metamorphoses*, vii. 157.

'But my time hieth fast', said King Arthur unto Sir Bedivere, 'Therefore take thou Excalibur my good sword, and goe with it unto yonder water side, and when thou commest there, I charge thee throw my sword into that water, and come againe and tell me what thou shalt see there.' . . . Then Sir Bedivere departed, and went to the sword, and lightly tooke it up, and went to the waters side; and there hee bound the girdell about the hilts, and then hee threw the sword into the water as farre as hee might; and there came an arme and an hand above the water, and met it and caught it, and so shooke it thrice and brandished.

But Prospero by his own deliberate act, without any intermediary, buries his staff and drowns his book.

It should now be plain why it was inevitable that the love-story should be secondary. Beside the fundamental energies realized in *The Tempest*, the lovers, who conform to the cycle of nature and belong to the world of pastoral, are destined to seem passive.[1] Ferdinand and Miranda are not conspicuously vital figure, sand Prospero never disguises that his most essential concern lies elsewhere, but they sufficiently represent the renewing experience of love in its first idyllic phase. *Chacun recommence le monde*: they are beginners both in their innocence and as the hope of the species, and Prospero fosters their courtship, just as he has nurtured and instructed his daughter, so that, when he subjects himself to the material cycle in its progression towards death, a continuing order will be preserved, and another beginning, another quest for fulfilment, will be assured. Having the open-mindedness of beginners, they are amenable to the forces within Prospero's realm which baffle the politicians and repudiate their time-worn formulas, so that even the moderate Gonzalo is finally desperate to quit:

> Some heavenly power guide us
> Out of this fearful country!

On the other hand, they are much too simple-minded and bemused to understand what is really happening on the island or what kind of drama is being enacted there.

[1] It is incumbent on those who make out that the love theme, or that of reconciliation and forgiveness, is centrally important to explain why these have attracted to themselves so little of the play's major poetry.

Now 'the charm dissolves apace', and it only remains to wind up issues in principle already settled. Ariel is dispatched on errands necessary for this purpose; Prospero, reconciled with Alonso, arranges to reassume state concerns and the task of preparing for death, when the wedding has been solemnized; and, subject to one last command to provide smooth seas, Ariel is restored to his own place:

> My Ariel, chick,
> That is thy charge: then to the elements
> Be free, and fare thou well!

And the island reverts to Caliban, its first lord. Whether or not the Epilogue which Prospero speaks at the end was meant to be understood as Shakespeare's farewell to the stage is unverifiable and also of little importance, since what matters is the central achievement of the play as a whole. *The Tempest* is the most complete realization which the form-giving process of imagination has achieved of its own nature and structure, and of its ambivalent relationship with the sources of its strength. It is the paradox of integrative power in dependence upon subversion at the heart of this process which imposes upon us and alone can reconcile our divergent ends: an assignment with the ever-fluctuating, an order that endures. And to realize it in concrete terms was for Shakespeare the only way of uniting the contrary ideals set forth in *Antony and Cleopatra* and *The Winter's Tale*. But, if Shakespeare's crowning accomplishment in *The Tempest* is to express the structure of imagination and its unitive function, what most of all makes his greatness, as we see it there, unique and fearful is that he conceives of the final return of power to its elemental origin, not as representing an insensible decline, but as being a deliberate action and a gift, as Rilke affirms in, it seems to me, the best criticism of *The Tempest* we have and the finest poem yet written on Shakespeare:

> ### The Spirit Ariel
> Sometime, somewhere, it had set him free,
> that jerk with which you flung yourself in youth
> full upon greatness, far from all respect.
> Then he grew willing: and since then a servant,

after each service waiting for his freedom.
Half-domineering, half almost ashamed,
you make excuses, that for this and this
you still require him, and insist, alas!
how you have helped him. Though you feel yourself
how everything that you detain in him
is missing from the air. Sweet and seductive,
to let him go, and then, abjuring magic,
entering into destiny like others,
to know that henceforth his most gentle friendship,
without all tension, nowhere bound by duty,
a something added to the space we breathe,
is busied thoughtless in the element.
Dependent now, having no more the gift
to form the dull mouth to that conjuration
that brought him headlong. Powerless, ageing, poor,
yet breathing *him* like infinitely wide
divided perfume making the Invisible
at last complete. Smiling, to think how once
your nod could bind him, now with such great acquaintance
grown so familiar. Perhaps weeping, too,
when you remember how he loved you and
desired to leave you, always both at once.
(And there I left it? Now he terrifies me,
this man who's duke again.—The way he draws
the wire into his head, and hangs himself
beside the other puppets, and henceforth
asks mercy of the play!...What epilogue
of achieved mastery! Putting off, standing there
with only one's own strength: 'which is most faint'.)

And yet, however carefully we seek to interpret Shakespeare's last plays in terms of poetic or thematic development, it will be with a degree of inconclusiveness *vis-à-vis* such alternative explanations as the contemporary vogue for romantic comedy and masque, unless we can support our view by some extrinsic comparison. As I shall now try to show, the needful parallel is to be found in the evolution of a painting which belongs to the same order of greatness as *The Tempest.*

III. *La Tempesta*

Giorgione is the only figure in Western literature or art whose mastery of the pastoral genre and poetic conception of it are strictly comparable to Shakespeare's. No critic has excelled Pater's intuitive appreciation of the qualities which affiliate Giorgione's ideal land scape both with myth and with the very greatest dramatic poetry:

> Now it is part of the ideality of the highest sort of dramatic poetry, that it presents us with a kind of profoundly significant and animated instants, a mere gesture, a look, a smile, perhaps—some brief and wholly concrete moment—into which, however, all the motives, all the interests and effects of a long history, have condensed themselves, and which seem to absorb past and future in an intense consciousness of the present. Such ideal instants the school of Giorgione selects, with its admirable tact, from that feverish, tumultuously coloured world of the old citizens of Venice—exquisite pauses in time, in which, arrested thus, we seem to be spectators of all the fulness of existence, and which are like some consummate extract or quintessence of life.

La Tempesta (Pl. 8), his finest work and one of five pictures that can be attributed to his hand with complete certainty, is beyond dispute one of the most wonderful and inexhaustible of all paintings. Its subject has been a mystery from the very beginning. Michiel, after he had seen the picture in 1530, set down in the forefront of his brief description, which mentions also a soldier[1] and a gipsy, 'A landscape with a tempest', and could provide no literary subject. There the matter has rested, despite much ransacking of classical literature for a suitable episode. Sir Kenneth Clark observes,

> The *Tempesta* is one of those works of art before which the scholar had best remain silent. No one knows what it represents; even Michiel, writing almost in Giorgione's day, could offer no better title than 'a soldier and a gypsy', and I think there is little doubt that it is a free fantasy, a sort of Kubla Khan, which grew as Giorgione painted it—for X-rays have shown us that Giorgione was an improviser, who changed his pictures as he went along, and that this composition

---

[1] It is now generally recognized that this figure is not a soldier.

Plate 8. Giorgione: *La Tempesta* (*Venice, Accademia*)

originally contained another naked woman, bathing her feet in the stream. This improvisation, which was so much at variance with studio practice of preceding painters, was characteristic of an art which was akin to lyric poetry. If we cannot say what the *Tempesta* means, still less can we say how it achieves its magical power over our minds.[1]

He maintains that the landscape puts us into 'that state of heightened emotion in which we can accept anything'. Although there is much to be said for the quietism he recommends, we cannot really afford to abandon the problem of what the painting signifies until we are absolutely certain that it is insoluble.

Giorgione took over the general structure of the composition and other important features from his earlier pastoral landscape, *The Finding of Paris*, now only preserved to us in a copy by Teniers (Pl. 9). The brook which diagonally bisects the composition, the stance of the shepherd on the right and the posture of his hand on the staff he lightly clasps, the position of the seated woman, the sharply broken-off cylindrical forms of the tree stumps, transformed in *La Tempesta* into columns and promoted to a central situation— all these were redeployed. The episode which is the subject of *The Finding of Paris* is to be found in Apollodorus, who tells how the child Paris was saved by the servant who had been entrusted with exposing him on Mount Ida:

and when a second babe was about to be born Hecuba dreamed she had brought forth a firebrand; and that the fire spread over the whole city and burned it. When Priam learned of the dream from Hecuba, he sent for his son Aesacus, for he was an interpreter of dreams, having been taught by his mother's father Merops. He declared that the child was begotten to be the ruin of his country and advised that the babe should be exposed. When the babe was born Priam gave it to a servant to take and expose on Ida; now the servant was named Agelaus. Exposed by him, the infant was nursed for five days by a bear; and, when he found it safe, he took it up, carried it away, brought it up as his own son on his farm, and named him Paris.[2]

---

[1] *Landscape into Art*, p. 58.
[2] Apollodorus, *Library*, III. xii. 5.

In Ovid's *Heroides*, xvi, Paris refers to this humble upbringing in narrating how Mercury brought him news of his elevation to serve as arbiter of beauty between Venus, Athena, and Juno, the role which gives him mythological importance. Although Giorgione's immediate subject is believed to have been suggested by a version of the story in Boccaccio's *Genealogy of the Gods*, the main source indicating a baby as a suitable centre-piece for an idyllic landscape was of course Virgil's deeply influential Fourth *Eclogue*, in which the wonder-child presides over the returned Golden Age:

> Enter—for the hour is close at hand—on your illustrious career, dear child of the gods, great increment of Jove. Look at the world, rocked by the weight of its over-hanging dome; look at the lands, the far-flung seas and the unfathomable sky. See how the whole creation rejoices in the age that is to be! ... Begin, then, little boy, to greet your mother with a smile: the ten long months have left her sick at heart. Begin, little boy: no one who has not given his mother a smile has ever been thought worthy of his table by a god, or by a goddess of her bed.[1]

Surely the most fundamental question is this: why was Giorgione impelled to revert to the composition of *The Finding of Paris* and to transform it as he did? The most obvious changes he made, the elimination of the old fluting shepherd in the bottom left-hand corner and the replacing of the two countrymen on the right by a single figure, provide a clue. Richter observes: 'the fact that the left hand corner figure is missing seems to prove that the artist now wishes to loosen the structural balance'.[2] Indeed yes. The interpretation of Shakespeare's final period we have advanced suggests a simple way of construing the same point: as for Shakespeare, the central figure of the abandoned baby, though in human terms an exceedingly open structure, *is yet not open enough*. Also, once more

---

[1] Our argument would support an explanation of the child's role in this most discussed of Latin short poems which has not enjoyed wide support as against political and Messianic theories: poetic necessity. Cf., for instance, the anti-monumental force of 'aspice convexo nutantem pondere mundum' as addressed to a child, and that of the moving reiterated petition, 'incipe, parve puer'. The little boy, the beginner, relieves the world of its oppressive solidity and weight.

[2] G. M. Richter, *Giorgio da Castelfranco* (1937), p. 79.

Plate 9. Teniers after Giorgione: *The Finding of Paris (formerly Florence, Loeser Collection)*

Plate 10. Bellini: *Sacred Allegory* (*Florence, Uffizi Gallery*)

as with Shakespeare, the pastoral idea must be superseded by a conception at once more severe and more comprehensive.

In *La Tempesta*, the richly dressed young man, fluent and easy of stance, poised to move on in a variety of possible directions to an unknown destination, palpably uncommitted and *vogelfrei*, pauses by the stream's edge. On the other side of it a woman, upon whose rough, simple features endurance has set its mark, is resting on the ground at the foot of a tree (its solidity contrasting with the ethereal lightness of the saplings on the left-hand side), anchored, committed and vulnerable, because of her bond with the child she suckles. For a moment the young man's glance is caught and directed towards her with an intense kind of detachment. In the landscape itself the sense of the marginal extreme is everywhere acute—in the stream which divides the composition, the line of medieval buildings receding towards a dark sky, the unfinished columns which end in air, the strange light which the storm disperses. Most of all in the light: it is an agreed technical fact that the composition is held together by this element which dissolves it. Following the same pattern of evolution as *The Tempest*, a pastoral idyll with an abandoned child as its central figure precipitates an altogether new form, a realization of the structure of imaginative activity itself. I do not suggest, for this would be misleading, that the painting represents the snake-encircled tree; rather, like *The Tempest*, it gives new definition to the dimensions within the human mind to which the component elements of that image correspond and to the function of the mind which unites them. On this view, Giorgione might be expected to break with inherited forms for the same reason as Shakespeare; and the two human figures would be, not representations of classical figures yet to be identified, but precisely what they now are—anonymous representations.

If this interpretation is correct, *La Tempesta* completes and brings full circle the most important phase in the evolution of Venetian poetic landscape. Its earliest major expression is generally acknowledged to be Bellini's *Sacred Allegory*,[1] (Pl. 10) painted in 1488 or thereabouts, and at one time attributed to Giorgione. The subject

[1] The painting was first described thus by Morelli in 1890.

of this picture was for a long time supposed to be derived from a fourteenth-century allegorical poem by Guillaume de Deguilleville, *Le Pèlerinage de l'âme*, but this is no longer believed to be a tenable interpretation.[1] The *Sacred Allegory* is now thought to be a landscape-fantasy organized around the idea of paradise;[2] and the design of the enclosure in the foreground is based on the traditional paradise-garden. Bellini's landscape has an unmistakably Hesperidean atmosphere, and to appreciate this fully we must remember how near to being interchangeable in their imaginative aspect as open and uncommitted structures, according to our argument, are child and snake. Despite the centaur on the further shore, the whole painting is instinct with that 'touching chastity' which marks all Bellini's incursions into material which even borders on the profane. On the left the virgin sits enthroned, flanked by two saints. Leaning on the marble parapet are St. Paul and St. Joseph, while on the right stand Job and St. Sebastian. But the imaginative centre of the painting, the point where its vitality is palpably concentrated, consists of a child clasping a tree, silhouetted against a break in the parapet where the enclave opens on to the water; and towards this configuration is directed the gaze of all figures in the composition who are not sunk in contemplative melancholia, apart from the averted St. Paul, as if they found it inexhaustibly satisfying. It is right that the summating masterpiece of the genre should define anew the idea set forth by the image at the centre of its first representative, and indeed it would have been most disappointing if it had done less.

In all basic respects *La Tempesta*, like *The Tempest*, does not belong to the vast proliferating tradition of imaginatively supine poetic and visual treatments of the ideal enclave, which, as well as being a source of needful refreshment, mirror the perennial human longing to retreat into the torpor of nature, even though they may take on a semblance of energy and depth from allegorical and Neoplatonic

[1] Ludwig advanced this explanation in 1902 and it met with general acceptance until 1946, when Rasmo advanced powerful arguments against it. See N. Rasmo, *La Sacra Conversazione degli Uffizi e il problema della sua comprensione* (Carro Minore, 1946).

[2] See W. Braunfels, 'Giovanni Bellinis Paradies-Gärtlein' in *Das Münster*, 1956.

trappings. This great pastoral inheritance, the legacy of Theocritus and Virgil, satisfying an ideal of harmony and repose, embracing a wealth of unexacting beauty and delight, is exemplified by such fantasies of secure and unsullied pleasure as the Cologne *Paradise-Garden*, and Spenser's Garden of Adonis in *The Faerie Queene*. Over against these stands a small group of masterpieces, for genius of a special order is needed, which do not seek to represent arcadian happiness but are, essentially, severe realizations of imaginative power, and so articulate the ideal form that its strength derives from the very elements making it unsustainable. *The Tempest* and *La Tempesta* represent this second immeasurably more profound and energetic type of ideality.

And so at last we are in a position to suggest an answer to the problem of Mercury's role in *Primavera*, with which this chapter began. In *Primavera*, as in *The Winter's Tale*, we see pastoral on the verge of breaking into another ideal mode. Mercury, a thief even in his infancy, as well as pointer to the Beyond, like Autolycus in Shakespeare's great romance, is a poetically necessary extra-cyclical element within the idyllic confine of the glade. He turns away with collected indolence from the subtly idealized but closed band of Graces at its centre. Idly skimming the clouds with his caduceus, tree and snake conjoined in miniature, embodying the divine power within the mind which he represents, he reaches with an expressiveness for which interpretation is no substitute towards the idyll's assignment with dissolving form. In him is discernible its thrust towards the kind of new development we see in *La Tempesta*.

4

PARADISE LOST

I

No poet was more acutely susceptible to the mysterious appeal of
the snake-encircled tree than Milton. My aim in now discussing
Paradise Lost is to show how his precise feeling for both the content
of the Greek Hesperides myth and that of the parallel Sumerian
myth of Inanna's Holy Garden broke the theoretical structure of
his epic, although this aspect of the poem has suffered from critical
preoccupation with other issues, in particular with Satan's heroic
role and claim to sympathy. We ought to have in mind at the outset
the most forcible illustration in his poetry of how minutely exact
this feeling was and of how enormously strong was the influence of
the Hesperides myth on Milton's imagination. It occurs in the
beautiful passage about the Hesperidean gardens omitted from the
opening speech of *Comus* in the published text but preserved in
the Trinity College Manuscript:

> Before the starrie threshold of Joves court
> my mansion is, where those immortall shapes
> of bright aereall spirits live insphear'd
> in regions mild of calme & serene aire
> amidst the [gardens] Hesperian gardens [on whose bancks]
>   [where the banks]
> [aeternall roses grow & hyacinth]
> bedew'd with nectar, & celestiall songs
> aeternall roses [grow] [yeeld] [blow] [blosme] grow & hyacinth
> & fruits of golden rind, on whose faire tree
> the scalie-harnest [watchfull] dragon ever keeps
> his [never charmed] uninchanted eye; & round the verge

& sacred limits of this [happie] blisfull Isle
the jealous ocean that old river winds
his farre-extended armes till wth steepe fall
halfe his wast flood ye wide Atlantique fills
& halfe the slow unfadom'd [poole of Styx] Stygian poole . . .

Milton retained only the first four lines, although he reincorporated vestiges of the deleted section in the Second Brother's speech:

But beauty like the fair Hesperian Tree
Laden with blooming gold, has need the guard
Of dragon watch with uninchanted eye,
To save her blossoms, and defend her fruit
From the rash hand of bold Incontinence.

Here the original 'scalie-harnest dragon' has become virtually unrecognizable, a grim *custos morum*; but coldness and dissociation are also discernible in the epithet 'uninchanted' which Milton substitutes in the final version of the draft for the intensely poetic 'never charmed'. His first choice of words almost duplicates the Sumerian phrase 'the snake who knows no charm'. Hesiod and Apollodorus, the most important Greek sources, use no comparable adjective. Ovid has 'unsleeping'. Other reading may or may not have had some influence, but for certain Milton had not read the Sumerian myths; and the verbal correspondence is at very least important prima-facie evidence in favour of the permanence that Blake ascribes to all such imaginative constructions, what Rosemond Tuve has called 'the stubborn logic of a great image'. Furthermore, Milton would not so watchfully have neutralized the allure of the serpent-guarded tree, if he could have exorcized from his thoughts that domain at the edge of the world, or the elements within his own mind which he found presented there. That he did not do so is shown by the strongly poetic evocation of the Hesperidean Garden at the end of *Comus*:

To the Ocean now I fly,
And those happy climes that ly
Where day never shuts his eye,
Up in the broad fields of the sky:

> There I suck the liquid ayr
> All amidst the Gardens fair
> Of *Hesperus*, and his daughters three
> That sing about the golden tree: . . .[1]

And by the deep nostalgia with which he recalls it in *Paradise Lost*,
when describing the stars glimpsed by Satan on his journey to earth:

> Or other Worlds they seemd, or happy Iles,
> Like those *Hesperian* Gardens fam'd of old,
> Fortunat Fields, and Groves and flourie Vales,
> Thrice happy Iles.[2] . . .

His paradise has generally been regarded as belonging to the great
miscellaneous tradition of ideal gardens and earthly paradises that
can be traced back to the garden of Alcinous in the *Odyssey*, in which
indeed it stands and to which it owes a great deal; but its true
prototype is the Garden of the Hesperides, and *Paradise Lost*, like
The Tempest and *La Tempesta*, is among the small group of energetic
treatments of the ideal enclave setting forth the structure of
imaginative activity which we have just distinguished from the
common stock of fundamentally torpid representations.

In *Paradise Lost*, we first view the new world where paradise is
situated through the eyes of Satan, as a minute haven of order
towards which he pursues his tremendous course through the
horrific region of chaos. Milton never more consummately represents energy as at once abounding and subtle than by his image
of Satan in the last phase of his journey, himself both sea and voyager:

> and *Satan* staid not to reply,
> But glad that now his Sea should find a shore,
> With fresh alacritie and force renewd
> Springs upward like a Pyramid of fire
> Into the wilde expanse, and through the shock
> Of fighting Elements, on all sides round
> Environd wins his way; harder beset
> And more endanger'd, than when *Argo* passd
> Through *Bosporus* betwixt the justling Rocks:

[1] 976–83.   [2] *P.L.* iii. 567–70.

Or when *Ulysses* on the Larbord shunnd
Charybdis, and by th'other whirlpool steard.
So hee with difficulty and labour hard
Mov'd on, with difficulty and labour hee . . .

Earth—'the happy isle' as Satan earlier describes it—is presented
as a containing shore to oceanic force, a strand perilously achieved
by the great forerunner of all whose passage lies along uncharted
coasts. Built into the imagined reality of Milton's paradise is the fact
that our earliest impression of it comes to us as we picture Satan
beating down upon it thus and not in some other way. After this
we cannot think of paradise as being land-locked. It is part of an
island exposed to a vast sea, the ocean that is Satan himself.

The great odyssey over and a landfall made, Satan sets foot at
last in paradise itself by leaping over the wall, not of necessity, but
to gratify his own impulse to break all such boundaries and
defences:

> One Gate there onely was, and that lookd East
> On th'other side: which when th' Arch-fellon saw
> Due entrance he disdain'd, and in contempt,
> At one slight bound high overleap'd all bound
> Of Hill or highest Wall, and sheer within
> Lights on his feet.

Milton likens Satan at this moment to a thief, who finds entry in
spite of the cautious householder's well-barred doors. And in full
knowledge of Mercury's celebrated theft on the evening of his first
day alive, although not perhaps in conscious recollection of it, he
adds,

> So clomb this first grand Thief into Gods Fould . . .

In thus presenting Satan as the archetypal thief, the precursor and
master of the other grand thieves of myth and literature, Milton
invests him with all the anti-geometrical associations of the thief in
his imaginative aspect. And thus he does justice to the same poetic
requirement that impelled Botticelli to incorporate the figure of
Mercury in *Primavera* and Shakespeare to include the thief Autolycus

in the pastoral section of *The Winter's Tale*. Nor is it just by entering
paradise in the role of celestial thief that Satan proclaims his opposition to all closed systems and static forms. Once arrived in Eden, his
first action, after declaring his envy, pity, and destructive intent, is
to give a virtuoso display of the divine power of metamorphosis by
transforming himself into one creature after another:

> Then from his loftie stand on that high Tree
> Down he alights among the sportful Herd
> Of those fourfooted kindes, himself now one,
> Now other, as thir shape servd best his end
> Neerer to view his prey, and unespi'd
> To mark what of thir state he more might learn
> By word or action markt: about them round
> A Lion now he stalkes with fierie glare,
> Then as a Tiger, who by chance hath spi'd
> In some Purlieu two gentle Fawnes at play,
> Strait couches close . . .

This protean exuberance fulfils no real tactical need, nor does the
plot demand it. Milton is using exactly the same device as Shakespeare does at a similar stage in the pastoral section of *The Winter's
Tale* to meet the poetic need, just as the idyll is taking shape, for
some momentary vista in which all formal possibilities seem open,
and meeting it in such a way as to establish at the same time Satan's
boundless formal versatility.

Yet Satan, whom we leave momentarily, is not the only element
in Book Four at odds with the idea of a closed system; for Milton,
once more like Shakespeare in *The Winter's Tale*, draws on the extra-
cyclical potential of the Persephone myth. The most haunting lines
in *Paradise Lost* have been duly recognized, without much attention
being paid to the causes or implications of their effect upon us, by
generations of readers:

> aires, vernal aires,
> Breathing the smell of field and grove, attune
> The trembling leaves, while Universal *Pan*
> Knit with the *Graces* and the *Hours* in dance
> Led on th' Eternal Spring. Not that faire field

Of *Enna,* where *Proserpin* gathring flours
Her self a fairer Floure by gloomie *Dis*
Was gatherd, which cost *Ceres* all that pain
To seek her through the World; nor that sweet Grove
Of *Daphne* by *Orontes* and th' inspir'd
Castalian Spring, might with this Paradise
Of *Eden* strive . . .

The image of Eternal Spring, the perpetual beginning before and outside the natural cycle, and the idea of a moment of primal liberty embodied in the Persephone myth (Milton is plainly led from one to the other by the suggestive power of Ovid's beautiful *perpetuum ver est*) give the same sudden sense of veering towards the extra-cyclical as the still greater lines on Proserpina in *The Winter's Tale* which we have already discussed. And it is the imperative need to counteract the oppressiveness of the idyllic confine, rather than the similarities between Proserpina and Eve so often remarked on, that precipitates the comparison of paradise to Proserpina's meadow and determines its exact rightness. Milton's sure and precise feeling for the Persephone myth is shown by the fact that the wonderful use of the double flower image, the flower-gatherer herself the flower gathered, likewise occurs in the passage from the Homeric *Hymn to Demeter*[1] quoted earlier, which Milton could not possibly have read,[2] because the one extant manuscript was only discovered in 1777. The primary effect of this poetry in its context, as of the idea of pre-cyclical freedom which it sets forth, is profoundly anti-paradisial: it devastates the illusion that a routine of mild gardening might under any conditions offer sustained felicity.

As an image, the ideal garden perennially beguiles us with its promise of secure happiness and ordered harmony; but to the indefinite *occupation* of gardens, not to speak of their care and

---

[1] νάρκισσόν θ', ὃν φῦσε δόλον καλυκώπιδι κούρῃ
Γαῖα Διὸς βουλῇσι (Hom. *Hymn Dem.* 8–9).
Lit. 'and the Narcissus which Earth brought forth at the will of Zeus as a snare for the girl with face like a budding flower'. The general idea of the *femme-fleur,* maiden as flower, occurs elsewhere (e.g. Catullus, lxii. 39–47) but not in the sharply poetic form it takes in the Homeric Hymn and in Milton.

[2] Except, possibly, ll. 417–19 and 474–6, cited by Pausanias, and l. 440, cited by Philodemus.

maintenance, there attaches a quite exceptional degree of tedium and restlessness. The most tactful poetic solution is to treat it as an unrealized possibility, a place which we are just on the point of occupying or which we might have occupied:

> Footfalls echo in the memory
> Down the passage which we did not take
> Towards the door we never opened
> Into the rose-garden.

Coleridge represents Kubla Khan as decreeing and laying out his pleasure-garden, but not as entering it. Milton, otherwise constrained by his source and epic purpose, embodies in his construction at every level the imaginative principle which must subvert it. His splendid baroque paradise, stately, verdurous, diversified with noble rivers, the epitome of the sure dispensation, would have been totally uncompelling without the satanic assault. The 'first grand Thief' not only breaks into the fold to destroy but at the same time energizes it and upholds it as an ideal form.

Nowhere is this more evident than in Milton's portrayal of the human inhabitants of paradise. Adam and Eve, inheritors of the garden which holds 'In narrow room Natures whole wealth', arouse a measure of nostalgia by their serene piety, the harmonious simplicity of their existence, the promise of a secure world which they enjoy; but their life, domesticated and cloistral, is only realized as poignantly enviable because of the extreme transience of their delight and first astonishment at their love and sufficiency for each other, and the impression of a momentary respite before a point of no return which Milton creates by counter-poised suggestions of progress and retreat:

> So pass'd they naked on, nor shunnd the sight
> Of God or Angel, for they thought no ill:
> So hand in hand they passd, the lovliest pair
> That ever since in loves imbraces met,
> *Adam* the goodliest man of men since borne
> His Sons, the fairest of her Daughters *Eve*.

His presentation of them is influenced everywhere by his realization that Shakespeare's words quoted a little earlier have a corollary:

everything that holds in perfection more than a little moment does
not grow. And the agent of the necessary development and change
is Satan.

Moreover, without Satan, Milton's treatment of Adam and Eve's
sexual relationship, far from happy as it is, would have been
disastrous:

> So spake our general Mother, and with eyes
> Of conjugal attraction unreprov'd,
> And meek surrender, half imbracing leand
> On our first Father, half her swelling Brest
> Naked met his under the flowing Gold
> Of her loose tresses hid: hee in delight
> Both of her Beauty and submissive Charms
> Smil'd with superior Love, as *Jupiter*
> On *Juno* smiles, when he impregns the Clouds
> That shed *May* Flowers; and pressed her Matron lip
> With kisses pure: aside the Devil turnd
> For envie, yet with jealous leer maligne
> Ey'd them askance, and to himself thus plaind.
> Sight hateful, sight tormenting! thus these two
> Imparadis'd in one anothers arms
> The happier *Eden*, shall enjoy thir fill
> Of bliss on bliss, while I to Hell am thrust,
> Where neither joy nor love, but fierce desire,
> Among our other torments not the least,
> Still unfulfill'd with pain of longing pines . . .

The love-making presented here would seem much more statuesque
and lacking in impetus than it does, if it were not energized by the
passionate force of Satan's commentary. His titanic despair com-
pensates for the very limited emotional register of Adam and Eve
at this stage. The intensity of his feeling helps to make up for the
undeveloped state of theirs, and without his vitalizing presence
they would seem flat and insubstantial. Nevertheless, a dark shadow
overhangs this episode, issuing from its whole poetic context, and
it is not Satan. Milton's technique of invocation by disavowed
comparison has been widely acknowledged in relation to the fabled

gardens of antiquity with which he so strongly associates paradise
by stressing how unlike them it is. The principle is one which
yields equally powerful negative effects. By gravely raising the
possibility of abstinence so as to dismiss it, and by insisting
laboriously on the innocence of our first parents' relations, he
establishes an imaginative link of the most harmful kind:

> nor turn'd I weene
> *Adam* from his fair Spouse, nor *Eve* the Rites
> Mysterious of connubial Love refus'd.

In bringing home to us that Adam did not renounce sex or turn
away from Eve, Milton introduces into our mind the thought that
he might very well have done so, and this spoils the impression of
something natural and inevitable. No less damaging is the way he
dissociates himself from an Augustinian view of sexuality in his
paean to wedded love:

> Farr be it, that I should write thee sin or blame,
> Or think thee unbefitting holiest place . . .

By pushing away all ideas of sinfulness and guilt Milton implies that
they are only too likely to be present, and so in effect brings them
nearer. It is these infiltrating suggestions of 'pale religious lechery'
that are the real threat to a sense of unalloyed ecstasy.

   While Eve sleeps, Satan, transforming himself to resemble a toad,
invades the anti-systematic region *par excellence*, the world of
fantasy and dreams. Even those who have never heard of Macrobius or *The Interpretation of Dreams*, let alone of the elaborate distinc-
tions by which troubled divines have sought to winnow the
inspired from the satanic, know the plainest fact about dreams: that
they disregard official prohibitions. In a single stream, commendable
and forbidden elements mingle so easily that no opposition is
detectable, least of all a combat between two mighty spirits.
Dreams do not conform to moral dualisms and ideal systems, and
are the Achilles heel of all Utopias and every kind of blue-print
laying down in advance how human life must be and what course it
must take. While applying himself to all this disruptive potential,

Satan is discovered by Gabriel's minions. There follows an elevated slanging match between him and Gabriel about the propriety and wisdom of breaking ordained limits. Satan, stung by the impudent foolishness of Gabriel's question as to why he has broken bounds, retorts,

> *Gabriel*, thou hadst in Heav'n th' esteem of wise,
> And such I held thee; but this question askt
> Puts me in doubt. Lives ther who loves his pain?
> Who would not, finding way, break loose from Hell,
> Though thither doomd?

To this he adds that the Omnipotent might at least be expected to guard his boundaries effectively:

> let him surer barr
> His Iron Gates, if he intends our stay
> In that dark durance . . .

At the height of this exchange a detachment of angels wheels into crescent formation and begins to surround him:

> While thus he spake, th' Angelic Squadron bright
> Turnd fierie red, sharpning in mooned hornes
> Thir Phalanx, and began to hemm him round
> With ported Spears, as thick as when a field
> Of *Ceres* ripe for harvest waving bends
> Her bearded Grove of ears, which way the wind
> Swayes them; the careful Plowman doubting stands
> Least on the threshing floore his hopeful sheaves
> Prove chaff. On th' other side *Satan* allarmd
> Collecting all his might dilated stood,
> Like *Teneriff* or *Atlas* unremov'd:
> His stature reachd the Skie, and on his Crest
> Sat horror Plum'd; nor wanted in his graspe
> What seemd both Spear and Shield . . .

This splendid manœuvre is abortive, for The Eternal himself intervenes, holding up a scale which bears the consequential advantages of conflict and separation. It tilts violently in favour of the second, and both parties defer to the celestial sign. The poetic importance of the episode is plain: it sustains and enlarges Satan's image as the mighty opposite of encircling forces.

II

As we know only too well, the treatment of the Fall itself presented Milton with an insuperable dilemma. The official view of man's pre-fallen status is defined by Augustine in a famous passage:

> For God had not made man like the angels in such a condition that even though they had sinned they could none the more die. He had so made them that if they discharged the obligation of obedience an angelic immortality and a blessed immortality might ensue without the intervention of death; but if they disobeyed, death should be visited on them as a just sentence.

Only an offence of the most heinous order could possibly call for so dreadful a punishment. But how could it have been committed, unless it sprang from needs and inclinations which an entirely good and completely fulfilled creature would not have? What kind of appeal could transgression present to wholly innocent beings? The eighth-century Northumbrian theologian Alcuin tried to meet this difficulty by suggesting that, even before the act of disobedience, Eve was less than perfect:

> Perhaps there was in her own mind a certain love of her own power and a certain proud presumption in it earlier than the temptation which should have been eliminated before the temptation.[1]

Yet Alcuin's hypothesis of faults and weaknesses before the Fall, although it makes the primordial crime much more understandable, in effect makes the Creator responsible for man's imperfections and entitles man to counter his maker's arraignment with the question, 'Why hast thou made me thus?' Man cannot justly be blamed or punished for the predictable outcome of his receiving at his creation a character and nature he never chose. On the other hand, if we suppose that there were no explanatory shortcomings or frustrations, the great offence becomes incomprehensible.[2]

---

[1] I owe this reference to Dr. J. M. Evans's thesis on the Fall of Man.

[2] A related difficulty should also be remembered here. The ban on tasting the fruit of the forbidden Tree of Knowledge is represented in *Paradise Lost* as not at all

Milton has to make his story coherent and intelligible, and yet his theoretical scheme does not allow him to cast doubt on man's perfection before the Fall. The compromise he in fact adopts is to blacken Eve's pre-fallen character as little as possible by making her total motive the sum of smaller frailties (or glimmers of enterprise). Restless for more diversity, she explains to Adam that gardening constantly together is inefficient and that by dividing their labour they could keep up better with the wanton pace at which paradisial foliage grows. Adam is filled with misgivings, knowing the malicious enemy waits to make an unspecified assault, but he has a hopeless case to argue. Solitude is a legitimate enjoyment; worse, he cannot press the idea that Almighty Wisdom allows traps and ambushes to be laid in the garden without eroding the idea of paradise itself, as Eve brings home to him with impeccable logic:

> If this be our condition, thus to dwell
> In narrow circuit strait'nd by a Foe,
> Suttle or violent, wee not endu'd
> Single with like defence, wherever met,
> How are we happie, still in fear of harm?

Even condescendingly:

> Let us not then suspect our happie State
> Left so imperfect by the Maker wise,
> As not secure to single or combin'd . . .

Meanwhile, Satan has returned at midnight from an intercontinental search for a suitable disguise, an adventure quite irrelevant to the furtherance of the main action but indispensable for preserving the sharpness of his image as voyager and explorer, his oceanic associations, and the sense of his quenchless energy:

> Sea he had searcht and Land
> From *Eden* over *Pontus*, and the Poole
> *Maeotis*, up beyond the River *Ob* . . .

difficult to comply with, an 'easy charge'. But this is sophistry, for we all know that one forbidden object in an enclosed space presents an irresistible attraction, and the one simple taboo, so far from being easy to observe, sets up a potent standing temptation.

> Downward as farr Antarctic; and in length
> West from *Orontes* to the ocean barrd
> At *Darien*, thence to the Land where flowes
> *Ganges* and *Indus* . . .

Having singled out the snake as the beast in whose form his wiles
will best merge with 'native subtlety', he has involved himself in
the mist that rises from a fountain close by the Tree of Life.
Resplendent, rearing his 'burnisht Neck of verdant Gold', he now
spirals towards Eve with all the compelling attractiveness of one
who skirts that marginal extreme of which, as Milton here makes
still plainer for us, the snake is the embodiment:

> With tract oblique
> At first, as one who sought access, but feard
> To interrupt, side-long he works his way.
> As when a Ship by skilful Stearsman wrought
> Nigh Rivers mouth or Foreland, where the Wind
> Veres oft, as oft so steers, and shifts her Saile;
> So varied hee, and of his tortuous Traine
> Curld many a wanton wreath in sight of *Eve*.

Now follow the two great sinuous temptation speeches, opening
with insidious flattery of Eve's beauty and the suggestion that
Paradise is a wretchedly provincial sphere of influence for what is
worthy of an audience of gods. Satan is careful to implant a compel-
lingly attractive image of the tree in Eve's mind before she knows
that it is in fact the forbidden one, explaining how by tasting its
fruit he has acquired wonderful new powers, reason, speech, and
the capacity to appreciate her loveliness. Then he leads her to the
tree, and his oratory gathers impassioned eloquence as he takes up his
most irresistible argument, which plays upon man's age-old suspicion
that the gods in their jealousy keep what is best for themselves:

> Why then was this forbid? Why but to awe,
> Why but to keep ye low and ignorant,
> His worshippers; he knows that in the day
> Ye Eate thereof, your Eyes that seem so cleere,
> Yet are but dim, shall perfetly be then
> Op'nd and cleerd, and yee shall be as Gods,
> Knowing both Good and Evil as they know.

Finally, having aroused these misgivings in Eve's mind, he offers as conclusive proof that the fruit is desirable the enlargement of life that has come to himself, without any ill effects, by eating it:

> look on mee,
> Mee who have toucht and tasted, yet both live,
> And life more perfect have attained then Fate
> Meant me, by ventring higher then my Lot.
> Shall that be shut to Man, which to the Beast
> Is op'n?

Might not the jealous overlord indeed have arbitrarily withheld from man some vast new potential? One safeguard might conceivably have availed at this point: an immediate knowledge of God. But this Eve lacks. Seventeenth-century Humanism has made him a distant absentee landlord of whom she knows only by hearsay, so that there is nothing evidently absurd in Satan's suggestion that the idea of a divine creation is an imposture and his alternative hypothesis about the origin of living things:

> The Gods are first, and that advantage use
> On our belief, that all from them proceeds;
> I question it, for this fair Earth I see,
> Warmd by the Sun, producing every kind,
> Them nothing . . .

Her loyalty to her maker has no basis in personal intercourse or affection, and thus her decision resolves itself into a calculation of probable risks. Surely, Eve reflects, the tree bears gifts a good maker would want his children to have. So she plucks the fruit, and death, with every kind of human ill, is unloosed:

> Earth felt the wound, and Nature from her seat
> Sighing through all her Works gave signs of woe,
> That all was lost.

It is difficult to find anything expressing with a grand simplicity equal to Milton's this most bitter of disappointed hopes, unless we go back to Siduri's disillusioning of Gilgamesh about his quest for immortality in the Babylonian *Epic of Gilgamesh*:

> Gilgamesh, where are you hurrying to? You will never find that life for which you are looking. When the gods created man they allotted to him death, but life they retained in their own keeping. . . . Let your clothes be fresh, bathe yourself in water, cherish the little child that holds your hand, and make your wife happy in your embrace; for this too is the lot of man.

In this catastrophe Kermode finds the heart of the poem:[1] 'So neer grows Death to Life.' It is the most profoundly realized moment in the work: concentrated in it, as well as grief over man's mortality, is all the pain of his setting forth from a state of simple harmony with his environment. Here Milton's feeling suddenly coincides with the element in the Genesis story itself which seems to have been least distorted by the attentions of redactors. But to take the poem at large as a great elegy with death as its subject would be, I think, to misconceive it.

Milton, as we have seen, chooses to make Eve's disobedience wholly credible at the cost of making any imputation of heinous guiltiness absurd. In fact he goes much further than this. As Adam realizes for the first time what Eve has done, and recovers himself sufficiently to break silence, Milton suddenly invests him with an entirely new depth of tenderness and another stature:

> O fairest of Creation, last and best
> Of all Gods Works, Creature in whom excelld
> Whatever can to sight or thought be formd,
> Holy, divine, good, amiable, or sweet!
> How art thou lost, how on a sudden lost,
> Defac't, deflourd, and now to Death devote?

Adam declares that, if Eve has to die, he is not to be parted from her and must share the same lot:

> som cursed fraud
> Of Enemie hath beguil'd thee, yet unknown,
> And mee with thee hath ruind, for with thee

---

[1] See *The Living Milton*, ed. F. Kermode (1960), pp. 117 ff.

Certain my resolution is to Die;
How can I live without thee, how forgoe
Thy sweet Converse and Love so dearly joind,
To live again in these wilde Woods forlorn?
Should God create another *Eve*, and I
Another Rib afford, yet loss of thee
Would never from my heart; no no, I feel
The Link of Nature draw me: Flesh of Flesh,
Bone of my Bone thou art, and from thy State
Mine never shall be parted, bliss or woe.

According to Milton's theoretical scheme, Adam shows culpable weakness here. He ought to have dissociated himself from Eve's crime, have refused to eat the same fruit, and thus have averted the second stage of the Fall. He was the victim of uxoriousness and feminine guile. But his nobility of utterance and feeling makes it quite impossible for us to respond in this censorious way and the humanist in us all hastens to side with the ways of man. When Adam has completed the Original Sin by eating the forbidden fruit, a strange exhilaration overcomes both him and Eve. Adam confesses that he feels intensity of passion he has never hitherto known, and for the second time in the poem they begin to make love, lying on a bed of flowers that recalls the scene of their earlier love-making:

For never did thy Beautie since the day
I saw thee first and wedded thee, adornd
With all perfections, so enflame my sense
With ardor to enjoy thee, fairer now
Then ever, bountie of this vertuous Tree.
  So said he, and forbore not glance or toy
Of amorous intent, well understood
Of *Eve*, whose Eye darted contagious Fire.
Her hand he seis'd, and to a shadie bank,
Thick overhead with verdant roof imbowr'd
He lead her nothing loath; Flours were the Couch,
Pansies, and Violets, and Asphodel,
And Hyacinth, Earths freshest softest lap.
There they thir fill of Love and Loves disport
Took largely, of thir mutual guilt the Seale,

> The solace of thir sin, till dewie sleep
> Oppressd them, wearied with thir amorous play.

Much ingenuity has been applied, mistakenly it seems to me, to detecting here a subtle decline from the allegedly rich and satisfying sexuality described earlier. Admittedly, Milton speaks just before this passage of 'carnal desire' and 'lascivious Eyes', deliberately invoking by means of these loaded phrases the notions of guilt which had overshadowed the earlier love-making by implication, and he follows it up with a devaluating commentary about forfeit of righteousness and native honour. And he gives this second love-making a certain atmosphere of feverishness. But the love play follows the same pattern as before, only desire is now urgent enough for Satan no longer to be needed in support, and an authentic current of feeling and mutual response more than make up for the loss of an essentially vacant serenity. Most important of all, it is plain that Adam and Eve have just discovered a profound human relationship for the first time. And this too is the work of Satan. If Satan is the destroyer of Adam and Eve's paradisial happiness, he is also the author of their new-found humanity.

The sudden unexplained outburst of mutual recrimination which occurs as soon as Adam and Eve awake, and which has no psychological coherence with what has gone before but is meant to establish that they have indeed fallen, marks the end of the paradisial state, although Adam and Eve have still to make the last reluctant exodus which closes the poem. The end of paradise itself is given in a tremendous prophetic description in Book Eleven:

> then shall this Mount
> Of Paradise by might of Waves be moovd
> Out of his place, pusht by the horned floud,
> With all his verdure spoild, and Trees adrift
> Down the great River to the op'ning Gulf,
> And there take root an Iland salt and bare,
> The haunt of Seales and Orcs, and Sea-mews clang . . .

The uncharted sea takes back into its vast desolation the idyllic design it has itself thrown up and for a while sustained as an ideal form. And so is completed another realization of the structure of imaginative activity after the pattern of *The Tempest*[1] and *La Tempesta*: the ideal enclave again draws an essential part of its strength from the force which requires and effects its dissolution, in this instance from the onslaught of Satan, the voyager who is himself an ocean. Like Shakespeare and Giorgione, Milton gives new definition to the unitive principle of the tree–snake configuration at the centre of the Hesperides myth, in other words to the function of the mind which reconciles those contrary dimensions within itself symbolized by tree and snake respectively. Milton's paradise presents its strongest and subtlest appeal to imagination, as do those earlier great works, by setting forth the paradox of integrative power in dependence upon subversion at the heart of its own form-giving process. And it is this process, as we have already said, which brings together the divergent modes of fulfilment we seek: to stand rooted in a continuing order and to frequent that marginal region where every form is but for the instant. The greatest poetry and art, amongst which *Paradise Lost* has a place, leave behind the pleasure-bound and passive conception of the earthly paradise, and are concerned to effect this all-important resolution.

Moreover, this achievement vitally affects our whole attitude and response to Milton's later poetry. We cannot here survey the long dispute about his status as a poet and his poetic style. Dr. Leavis's influential and sweeping indictment resolves itself into two main counts: first, that Milton's later work is remote from myth, un-Shakespearian, a product of the indomitable will; second, that the poetry is monumental at the expense of vitality and suppleness. Here is Leavis on the first count, with which I am mainly concerned:

But it is enough to point to the limitations in range and depth of Milton's interests, their patent inadequacy to inform a 'sense of myth, of fable, of ordered wholes in experience'. His strength is of the kind that we indicate when, distinguishing between intelligence and

---

[1] We know that Milton was in fact deeply influenced by *The Tempest* from the echoes of it in *Comus* often remarked upon by commentators.

character, we lay the stress on the latter; it is a strength, that is, involving sad disabilities.[1]

And again:

Milton's inadequacy to myth, in fact, is so inescapable, and so much is conceded in sanctioned comment, that the routine eulogy of his 'architectonic' power is plainly a matter of mere inert convention.[2]

This ascription to Milton of an essentially unpoetic highmindedness has, I believe, done far more damage to Milton's reputation than Leavis's attack upon the Grand Style. Our analysis of Milton's style must to a large extent map out and rationalize an earlier non-analytic reaction to his poetry. And the suggestion that Milton is inadequate to myth, in other words to the most basic kind of poetry, works at this decisive pre-articulate level with lethal effect. To miss how near Milton is to myth, as well as to Shakespeare, is to be insulated from the full impact of his poetic energy, and so from his greatness. And we ought to remember here that the famous judgement of Blake, 'He was a true Poet and of the Devil's party without knowing it', did not refer to Milton's moral sympathies but was addressed to the decisive issue of poetic energy. The whole argument of *The Marriage of Heaven and Hell* makes it certain that, in declaring this, Blake was asserting the very opposite of the view that Milton's essential greatness was one of character. In allying Milton with devils, he was opposing the abundance and unexpectedness of genius to the fixity of angels, who are bound by analytics and systematic reasoning, so placing him *vis-à-vis* one of the central ideas of *The Marriage of Heaven and Hell*, the antithesis expressed by the proverb 'The cistern contains, the fountain overflows.' 'Devils are various, Angels are all alike.' Blake was acknowledging that Milton possessed in highest degree the imaginative energy which distinguishes great poetry and reverses the drift towards inertia of mere ratiocination and sensibility.

It has to be conceded as a truism that the gulf in *Paradise Lost* between official theme and achieved effect destroys at least one possible kind of unity. But this leaves entirely open its status as a work of art, because there is no epic where avowed intent and

---

[1] *Revaluation* (1936), p. 58.
[2] Op. cit., p. 59.

accomplishment break asunder in this manner or on this scale, and so we have no standards of assured relevance. A sound theoretical case can be made for holding this particular breach between aim and execution to be either a catastrophic flaw or a singular manifestation of strength; consequently we are able to rationalize our instinctive reaction to the work by evaluating the importance of unity in almost any way that suits us. Obviously too, but for Milton's Christianity we should be spared the many perfunctory yet hurtful wrenchings of the theological rudder that are distributed throughout the poem; and it might fairly be argued that in seeking to bring into relief what seems to me its imaginative centre I have given no sense of the length or rotundity of sections of the work in which Milton unequivocally supports and all too painstakingly sets forth official doctrine, an omission amply made good in other criticism of *Paradise Lost*. Against such shortcomings of Milton's epic, however, must be set, among other things, the very great improbability that the tremendously important and recalcitrant story of the Fall could have been explored by major genius except at such a price. And in the history of the European imagination over the last four hundred years Milton's poetic achievement is only of lesser significance than the terrible new appraisal made in *King Lear* of a cosmos no longer felt to be ordered for the good of man. The doctrine of the Fall, justifying God's ways and exonerating him from responsibility for the manifest evils and imperfections of the world, was the principal bastion of the traditional structure, and a more tenacious belief, being rooted in ancient feelings of guiltiness before the gods, nurtured by centuries of Christian and pre-Christian teaching. Milton broke this idea at a level accessible only to one passionately convinced of its truth, mainly through his deep awareness of myth and the poetic subtlety of his presentation of Satan. He not only laid bare the incoherence of the official theodicy but, against all reasonable odds, extended a great tradition of mythopoeic thought, assimilating and transforming the largely alien story of the lost garden of supine delight, imposing upon it a truly imaginative mode of ideality; and only the disturbing relevance of *Paradise Lost* to our present state can foster for long any hope of fencing it off as a literary monument.

5

COLERIDGE:
'THE ANCIENT MARINER'
AND 'KUBLA KHAN'

I

WE find in Coleridge the same preoccupation with the types of ideal form that we have been considering as in Shakespeare and Milton, but without their masterful and sure control. For instance, although Coleridge is irresistibly attracted by the idea of the marginal extreme, it has for him an ambience of fearfulness that is missing in Shakespeare and Milton:

> I fear thee, ancient Mariner!
> I fear thy skinny hand!
> And thou art long, and lank, and brown,
> As is the ribbed sea-sand.

This has the paradoxical advantage that his poetry makes more evident how formidable is the task of reconciling the dimensions of thought and feeling represented by tree and snake, more plain how great are those who have accomplished it. But not only does Coleridge extend and illuminate our theme. The mythical tradition we have been examining in turn throws light on the most fundamental problems that arise from his two greatest poems. It explains the basic structure of *The Ancient Mariner*, and I believe it helps to bridge the gulf between Coleridge's critics who have for the most part asserted, rightly it seems to me, that *Kubla Khan* is a self-sufficient poem, and Coleridge's own belief, expressed in the celebrated note about interruption by the 'person on business from

Porlock', and elsewhere, that he had failed to execute a greater design. It also enables us to understand the organizing principle within the nexus of thought and reading about the sea and the motif of paradise from which these poems issued in successive years. In case the reader should need more instantaneous assurance of Coleridge's relevance to what has gone before, it should be added that, as well as being of all our post-Renaissance poets the most steeped and versed in Neoplatonic speculation, he was also familiar (from his reading of Dupuis)[1] with the belief that the Southern polar region was the zone which belonged to the planet Mercury. But first we must recall with some particularity the main events of *The Ancient Mariner*.

An old sailor who has spent his life on the great waters accosts a 'gallant', as he is about to attend the reassuring occasion *par excellence*, a wedding-feast, and compels him to hear out his dreadful tale. It begins abruptly with the setting forth of a ship and its crew in a mood of carefree expectancy, as the last outpost of the human and institutional order disappears from sight:

> The ship was cheered, the harbour cleared,
> Merrily did we drop
> Below the kirk, below the hill,
> Below the lighthouse top.

Day after day, the sun rises and sets with seemingly benign regularity, and the storm blast chases them ever southward into a region strange, fearsome, and beautiful:

> And now there came both mist and snow,
> And it grew wondrous cold:
> And ice, mast-high, came floating by,
> As green as emerald.

And, while they are bewildered amidst the omnipresent ice, there comes winging through the snow-fog a great sea-bird, for whom the ice fields are a native region. We only know of the creature that it appears on its way to a destination of its own and that these

---

[1] See J. L. Lowes, *The Road to Xanadu* (1951 ed.), p. 236.

foggy and trackless wastes present no threat to it. For a time the Albatross attaches itself to the ship and crew as preserver and guide, so that they are able to begin to steer their way northward again. But suddenly the Mariner commits the dreadful and decisive act:

> 'God save thee, ancient Mariner!
> From the fiends, that plague thee thus!
> Why look'st thou so?'—'With my cross-bow
> I shot the ALBATROSS.'

There follows an uncertain interim, raising the illusory hope that there may after all be no fatal repercussions. According to the vagaries of the weather, the fickle shipmates first denounce the shooting of the bird, and a short time afterwards applaud it. Then the Albatross begins to be avenged by an utterly dreadful inertia, torment by heat and thirst, the sight of the rotting deep, a loathing which supplants all other responses, the febrile colour-sensations of nightmare, the drying up of the very sources of articulation. And the Mariner's fellow sailors hang the dead sea-bird round his neck as a sign of his guilt:

> Ah! well a-day! what evil looks
> Had I from old and young!
> Instead of the cross, the Albatross
> About my neck was hung.

The sense of irremediable loss is even more immediate than any we associate with sacrilege against some tremendous sanctity.

Now there bears down from westward an unidentifiable boat, tacking and veering; and the Mariner makes his first and last desperate attempt to act in self-preservation:

> Through utter drought all dumb we stood!
> I bit my arm, I sucked the blood,
> And cried, A sail! a sail!

The result is disaster: he precipitates the unavertable, the surrender of himself and his companions into the power of two fantasms, Death and The Nightmare Life in Death, who dice for victims, the more horrible of them winning for herself the guilty one. It is at this moment that the Wedding Guest utters his most memorable cry of fear and revulsion, shrinking from the Mariner as from a thing washed by the primordial and unfathomable sea.

The Mariner endures an anguish of guilt, with his dead companions at his feet expressing by their eyes the curse they cannot speak. But no less terrible is his loneliness and the total drought devastating the innermost springs of feeling. With envy and immense longing he looks towards the moon and the stars, coolly and serenely moving up the sky in effortless progress through their native domain, and it is important to notice that, although the moon is not positively malign like the sun, she only offers mockery:

> Her beams bemocked the sultry main,
> Like April hoar-frost spread;
> But where the ship's huge shadow lay,
> The charmed water burnt alway
> A still and awful red.

At this instant, when every resource and initiative of his own have failed him, there break into a situation of seemingly perpetual fixity the water-snakes, as ever destroyers of set form, untransfixed by the 'charmed' water:

> Within the shadow of the ship
> I watched their rich attire:
> Blue, glossy green, and velvet black,
> They coiled and swam; and every track
> Was a flash of golden fire.

For no reason he can understand he blesses the snakes in his heart:

> A spring of love gushed from my heart,
> And I blessed them unaware:
> Sure my kind saint took pity on me,
> And I blessed them unaware.

And his deliverance begins:

> The self-same moment I could pray;
> And from my neck so free

> The Albatross fell off, and sank
> Like lead into the sea.

The gradual restoration of the Mariner is now expressed by a
number of images of returning life, and two fellow daemons of the
polar spirit (who, were we determined to identify him, would have
to be Mercury) debate whether or not the offender has suffered
enough, in view of his irreversible offence against an object of that
spirit's love:

> The spirit who bideth by himself
> In the land of mist and snow,
> He loved the bird that loved the man
> Who shot him with his bow.

The Mariner is subjected to a last phase of guilt and suffering, and
then released. Then with unspeakable joy he sees once more his
native land, its beacon and its kirk. He is back within the sphere of
charts and inherited knowledge, where also the ministrations of
traditional religion are efficacious: hitherto the sanctity of good
and holy men would not have availed, even had they been accessible.
The boat, visible reminder of his agony, sinks into the depths, and
he is shriven by the hermit in token of his reconciliation with God
and human society; and yet he will always bear his scars and the
marks of having entered a desolate region unknown to ordinary
men:

> O Wedding-Guest! this soul hath been
> Alone on a wide wide sea:
> So lonely 'twas, that God himself
> Scarce seemèd there to be.

And from the depths of that terrible experience he commends to the
Wedding Guest before they separate, presumably for ever, a few
sentiments, trite in any other circumstances, about the value of
piety, church-going, the familiar, love of all created things; but this
does not make his impact less devastating on one whose knowledge
has been confined to the familiar world, for the Wedding Guest
departs like a man who has been pole-axed:

> He went like one that hath been stunned,
> And is of sense forlorn:
> A sadder and a wiser man,
> He rose the morrow morn.

I shall concentrate upon three problems raised by this intensely mysterious poem, all of them questions which on any view must be central to its understanding. Why does the Wedding Guest react to the Mariner with a para-normal degree of fear? Why is there an atmosphere of nightmare, controlled to the extent that it is expressed, of that very specific kind of dream which grips us in an unresponding fixity, and etymologically, as in veritable fact, represents an assault by the feminine principle? And what is the precise significance of the shooting of the Albatross?

The most promising way of approaching this group of questions is to consider the most entrancing and poignantly beautiful lines in *The Ancient Mariner*,

> The moving Moon went up the sky,
> And no where did abide:
> Softly she was going up,
> And a star or two beside . . .

They distil the feeling for moonlight which pervades so much of Coleridge's work, and to which he assigns such great importance in his account of the inception of *Lyrical Ballads*:

the sudden charm, which accidents of light and shade, which moonlight or sun-set diffused over a known and familiar landscape... These are the poetry of nature.[1]

Contrast with Coleridge's quatrain Cleopatra's reference to the moon in a passage quoted earlier,

> the odds is gone,
> And there is nothing left remarkable
> Beneath the visiting moon.

Shakespeare sharply redresses the enveloping softness inseparable from the idea of the moon, immemorially associated with femininity,

---

[1] *Biographia Literaria*, Ch. xiv.

by stressing distinction and difference: but Coleridge embraces the image for the very reason that it extinguishes minute determinations. Ironically enough it was the description of the moon in *The Ballad of Sir Patrick Spens* ('I saw the new moon late yestere'en / wi' the auld moon in her arm') which precipitated the Dejection Ode with its confession that he has lost his 'Shaping Spirit of Imagination'. Coleridge analyses the cause of this terrible deprivation in the stanza of the Ode immediately preceding the one in which he so memorably describes the loss itself:

> Thou need'st not ask of me
> What this strong music in the soul may be!
> What, and wherein it doth exist,
> This light, this glory, this fair luminous mist,
> This beautiful and beauty-making power.
>   Joy, virtuous Lady! Joy that ne'er was given,
> Save to the pure, and in their purest hour,
> Life, and Life's effluence, cloud at once and shower,
> Joy, Lady! is the spirit and the power,
> Which, wedding Nature to us, gives in dower
>   A new Earth and new Heaven,
> Undreamt of by the sensual and the proud:
> Joy is the sweet voice, Joy the luminous cloud . . .

And this diagnosis is expanded in a despairing entry in the Note Book for 1803 (*C.N.*, 1609):

I write melancholy, always melancholy: You will suspect that it is the fault of my natural Temper. Alas! no.—This is the great Occasion that my Nature is made for Joy—impelling me to Joyance—& I never, never can yield to it.—I am a genuine *Tantalus*—[1]

Immeasurable is the gulf in experience and understanding between the self-deceiving childishness of this lament for lost Joy and Blake's aphorism in *Auguries of Innocence*,

---

[1] Coleridge's assessment has been too readily accepted; e.g. 'As Wordsworth saw, the condition which Coleridge required for this spontaneous creative activity was a kind of happiness which health and his unfulfilled affections denied him. As the Dejection Ode itself made terribly clear, the essential Joy was missing' (Humphry House, *Coleridge* (1953), p. 156).

> Man was made for Joy and Woe;
> And when this we rightly know
> Thro' the World we safely go.

For not only Coleridge's pathetic reliance on Joy as a loadstone and panacea, but his whole life and work, declare him a victim of that destructive passivity into which Nature lures all who trust her too much or court her unwarily, and which Blake, who understood the radical sleepiness of Nature and her power, gradually and without our knowing it, to lower our level of awareness, realized again and again in his poetry, but most strongly at the end of *Songs of Innocence and Experience* in the lines addressed to Tirzah, who here personifies 'the delusive goddess Nature' herself:

> Thou Mother of my Mortal part,
> With cruelty didst mould my Heart,
> And with false self-deceiving tears
> Didst bind my Nostrils, Eyes, and Ears. . . .

We need to remember in this connection other lines in *The Ancient Mariner* where Coleridge weaves a spell of the same kind as in the verse about the moon and the stars:

> The many men, so beautiful!
> And they all dead did lie . . .
>
> Oh sleep! it is a gentle thing,
> Beloved from pole to pole!
> To Mary Queen the praise be given!
> She sent the gentle sleep from Heaven,
> That slid into my soul.

And we should notice how strongly can be felt in them the appeal of that seductive torpor which is for Blake the ultimate enemy.

In Coleridge's critical theory Imagination represents formulative activity of the most energetic kind, what he calls 'the *modifying* Power in that highest sense of the word in which I have ventured to oppose it to Fancy, or the *aggregating* power'.[1] Yet throughout his prose-writing we find the same drift towards an ideal of merging the distinct and particular in the indeterminate that is reflected in

---

[1] *C.L.* ii. 1034.

The Ancient Mariner, and a constant tendency to propound and think in terms of those cloudy general notions which Blake, for whom art has its life in severe and minute particulars, saw as sure symptoms of imaginative enfeeblement, a capitulation to nature, a readiness merely to classify and to rearrange, and so in effect to repeat, what has happened all too often before. And since Coleridge and Blake, as well as being both major poets, were both impelled by analytic dispositions to consider imagination in its theoretical aspect and in relation to a considered ideal of knowledge and understanding, let us pursue here a little more systematically the tendency to refer to Blake that has already surfaced at intervals. In his letter to John Thelwell of 14 October 1797, Coleridge expresses his longing to escape from the intolerable burdensomeness of the world of particular forms into an undifferentiated mode of awareness:

I can *at times* feel strongly the beauties you describe, in themselves, and for themselves—but more frequently *all things* appear little—all the knowledge, that can be acquired, child's play—the universe itself—what but an immense heap of *little* things?—I can contemplate nothing but parts, and parts are all *little*—!—My mind feels as if it ached to behold and know something *great*—something *one and indivisible*—and it is only in the faith of this that rocks or water-falls, mountains or caverns give me the sense of sublimity or majesty![1]

Blake, on the other hand, declares,

it is in Particulars that Wisdom consists & Happiness too.[2]

Again, compare Coleridge's idea of the sublime with Blake's. Here is Coleridge:

Where neither whole nor part, but unity as boundless or endless allness—the sublime.[3]

And here Blake:

All Sublimity is founded on Minute Discrimination.[4]

About 10 March 1798, Coleridge writes to his brother George,

[1] *C.L.* i. 349.   [2] K. 611.
[3] T. Allsop, *Letters, Conversations and Recollections of S.T. Coleridge* (1836), p. 197.
[4] K. 453.

I have for some time past withdrawn myself almost totally from the consideration of *immediate* causes, which are infinitely complex and uncertain, to muse on fundamental and general causes—the '*causae causarum*'.[1]

Contrast with this Blake's attitude to generalization, expressed apropos of Reynolds's observation that the power to abstract and generalize is 'the great glory of the human mind':

> To Generalize is to be an Idiot. To Particularize is the Alone Distinction of Merit. General knowledges are those Knowledges that Idiots possess.[2]

Or let us take Coleridge's observation, 'a Poet's Heart and Intellect should be *combined, intimately* combined and *unified* with the great appearances in Nature',[3] and place against it Blake's criticism of Wordsworth, the severest verdict ever delivered on Romantic poetry in general. Against Wordsworth's statement 'the powers requisite for the production of poetry are, first, those of observation and description, second Sensibility', Blake writes,

> One Power alone makes a Poet: Imagination, The Divine Vision.[4]

Beside the title to a passage from *The Prelude* that Wordsworth published separately, *The Influence of Natural Objects in calling forth and strengthening the Imagination in Boyhood and early Youth*, he writes,

> Natural Objects always did & now do weaken, deaden & obliterate Imagination in Me. Wordsworth must know that what he Writes Valuable is Not to be found in Nature.

Blake's comment on the relation between Imagination and Nature, as well as being relevant to Coleridge, is of fundamental importance for our understanding of the whole romantic movement. The undoing of many of the Romantic poets,[5] and it could easily be ours, was that in reacting against rationalism they too uncritically espoused passivity. Among English Romantic poets none was more

---

[1] *C.L.* i. 397.　　　　　　　　　　　　　　　[2] K. 451.
[3] *C.L.* ii. 864.　　　　　　　　　　　　　　　[4] K. 782.
[5] Keats was, of course, a notable exception. Throughout the *annus mirabilis* of 1818–19 he was engaged in working out a more severe alternative ideal to that of identifying himself with the realm of 'Flora and Old Pan'.

deeply implicated in that tragic mistake than Coleridge, for, although in theory Imagination was for him above all an active power, the true bent of his own imagination, as I hope soon to make still plainer, ran quite counter to his beliefs about this faculty.

However, despite all the signs in Coleridge's poetry and prose of a flawed imaginative endowment,[1] two broad assumptions about him have enjoyed virtual supremacy since his own lifetime. In the first place, it has been taken for granted that his capacity for execution failed to match his ability to conceive. Hazlitt wrote of him, 'he could not realise all he knew or thought',[2] and other critics have echoed him, deliberately or otherwise, ever since.[3] Secondly, it has almost always been regarded as obvious that for a brief period at least Coleridge possessed imaginative vitality of the highest order. We must now approach *Kubla Khan* alert to the possibility that both these suppositions may be invalid, and that what we really find throughout Coleridge's poetry, judged by the severest standards— for his wonderful intellect and sensitivity, massive complexity, and the narrowness by which he missed the heights of greatness call for no less—are an imperfect power to conceive and an innate bias towards torpid imaginative forms; and then we may be in a position to frame provisional answers to our three questions about *The Ancient Mariner*.

II

It will be convenient to have *Kubla Khan* before us:

> In Xanadu did Kubla Khan
> A stately pleasure-dome decree:
> Where Alph, the sacred river, ran
> Through caverns measureless to man
> Down to a sunless sea.

[1] To recognize this does not commit us to the proposition that Coleridge was, with all the condescending overtones of the phrase, 'a failure'.
[2] In *The Spirit of the Age*.
[3] e.g. 'he could conceive where he could not execute...' (E. L. Griggs (ed.), *Collected Letters* (1956), Introduction, p. xxxiii) and the late Professor Garrod's moving comparison of Coleridge's poetry to an unfinished cathedral in his Introduction to the Clarendon Press edition.

So twice five miles of fertile ground
With walls and towers were girdled round:
And there were gardens bright with sinuous rills,
Where blossom'd many an incense-bearing tree;
And here were forests ancient as the hills,
Enfolding sunny spots of greenery.

But O! that deep romantic chasm which slanted
Down the green hill athwart a cedarn cover!
A savage place! as holy and enchanted
As e'er beneath a waning moon was haunted
By woman wailing for her demon-lover!
And from this chasm, with ceaseless turmoil seething,
As if this earth in fast thick pants were breathing,
A mighty fountain momently was forced:
Amid whose swift half-intermitted burst
Huge fragments vaulted like rebounding hail,
Or chaffy grain beneath the thresher's flail:
And 'mid these dancing rocks at once and ever
It flung up momently the sacred river.
Five miles meandering with a mazy motion
Through wood and dale the sacred river ran,
Then reach'd the caverns measureless to man,
And sank in tumult to a lifeless ocean:
And 'mid this tumult Kubla heard from far
Ancestral voices prophesying war!
    The shadow of the dome of pleasure
    Floated midway on the waves;
    Where was heard the mingled measure
    From the fountain and the caves.
It was a miracle of rare device,
A sunny pleasure-dome with caves of ice!

A damsel with a dulcimer
In a vision once I saw:
It was an Abyssinian maid,
And on her dulcimer she played,
Singing of Mount Abora.
Could I revive within me

> Her symphony and song,
>   To such a deep delight 'twould win me,
> That with music loud and long,
> I would build that dome in air,
> That sunny dome! those caves of ice!
> And all who heard should see them there,
> And all should cry, Beware! Beware!
> His flashing eyes, his floating hair!
> Weave a circle round him thrice,
> And close your eyes with holy dread,
> For he on honey-dew hath fed,
> And drunk the milk of Paradise.

With interpretations which take this poem to be a self-sufficient treatment either of imaginative failure or of the fusion of pleasure and sacredness I have no quarrel. Regarded as a major treatment of the ideal enclave, its deficiencies are of the most fundamental kind. That there is no sustained occupation of the pleasure-dome by Kubla is an evasion of the central problem. Coleridge offsets the oppressiveness of girdling walls and towers by disruptive elements, the sacred river and the ominous voices; but he shies away from making them effectively sharp. The river pursues a hesitantly circuitous course; the caverns into which it flows are 'measureless' but unexplored, the ancestral voices distant and indeterminate. Furthermore, why a 'lifeless' ocean? Perhaps Coleridge felt that one real ocean, the sea of *The Ancient Mariner*, was more than enough. And the damsel with the dulcimer whose song might have made Coleridge the dread seer who has entered and possessed the paradisial region? Is he not projecting upon her and upon her instrument that 'strong music of the soul' which he craves in the 'Dejection' Ode, his siren-affair with Joy, his delusion that it might solve all problems? The imaginative drowsiness of the poem is inestimably more important than the 'two grains of opium' that influenced it.

Although I offer this suggestion with some tentativeness, I believe that Coleridge knew his poem's limitations, was aware that a greater theme had served a summons on him, and that this

was why he insisted in the note added to the autograph copy of
Kubla Khan, now in the British Museum, that it was 'a fragment,
with a good deal more, not recoverable'. For, even if it may be
wrong to regard *Kubla Khan* as an incomplete or unsuccessful
poem, it is still necessary to ask why Coleridge never came
nearer than this to actualizing on a major scale a theme which was
constantly in his thoughts. Why did he stop short at a pleasure-
fantasy which, although much finer than, say, *This Limetree Bower
My Prison*, whose title epitomizes Coleridge's dilemma, remains
little more than the most distinguished product of the English-
man's centuries-old Oedipal love-affair with artificial and natural
landscape, the inheritance which eventually devolves upon Housman?

To have written a great poem on the ideal enclave would, according to our argument, have demanded a new realization of imaginative power, setting forth once more the unitive principle of the
tree–snake configuration, in other words the function of the mind
that reconciles those contrary ideals which tree and snake present
to us; and Coleridge was incapable of that achievement. For the
fear which obtains in *The Ancient Mariner* between the Wedding
Guest, who embodies our life in its tree-like aspect, bound for the
feast that celebrates the rightness of the familiar order and man's
enduring trust that his seed may inherit the land, and the sea-
wanderer who has learnt at a dreadful price to bless the water-snakes
in his heart, confirms, as it expresses, this very inability.[1] To fail
here and yield to an ideal of passivity was to surrender awareness

---

[1] For a more abstract treatment of this relationship and of our main theme I would
refer the reader to Eliot's *Four Quartets*. The first Quartet, *Burnt Norton*, explores the
motif of the paradisial garden. But the two middle Quartets are occupied with the
dimensions of the mind represented by tree and snake, the world of Cleopatra and
that of *The Winter's Tale*, Mariner and Wedding Guest. At the end of *East Coker*, which
treats of the immemorial cycle of generation, and indeed opens with the image of a
dance 'signifying matrimonie', we are bidden to move out into 'the vast waters of the
petrel and the porpoise'. At the close of *The Dry Salvages*, whose principal theme is
Ocean, and the last outpost of the human order in the midst of it (the bell), we are
counselled to remain 'not too far from the yew-tree'. Central to the poem is the idea
of the unitive role of the poet's art and its fundamental complicity with subversion.
Despite the special reference to the dilemma of the poet, the subject at large is, of
course, the consummation of the whole imaginative life.

and severe articulation to the enveloping forces which assert themselves in nightmare; and any surrender of this kind damages or
destroys the alert and volatile principle which, whatever name we
give it, is the mediator between us and the uncharted waters: it is
as if we were to shoot an albatross.

Finally, lest an explanation of Coleridge's failure in terms of
dissociation between tree and snake, a falling apart of those elements
in the mind to which they correspond, should seem to be the kind
of sweeping idea which cannot be roped down by hard evidence,
let us turn to the 1795–9 Note Book, the document on the basis of
which J. L. Lowes, in his fine genetic inquiry, *The Road to Xanadu*,
argues that *The Ancient Mariner* is 'a work of pure imagination', but
which, it seems to me, conclusively shows the very opposite to be
the case.

III

There are two potentially rewarding ways of approaching the
1795–9 Note Book, from now on referred to as the Note Book, to
deal with it either at great length, as Lowes does in *The Road to
Xanadu*, or selectively and intensively; and it is the second method
that I shall adopt here. The Note Book, discontinuous and wide-
ranging though it is, exhibits a fundamental pattern: the to-and-fro
movement of Coleridge's mind between the motif of Ocean and his
need to retreat from it and spin for himself a narcotizing cocoon. On
page forty-four he notes the verse from Isaiah (*C.N.* 239),

Thou wilt keep him in perfect peace whose mind is stayed on thee
because he trusteth in thee.

But in fact, as we shall see, the Note Book confirms that at the
heart of Coleridge's need for Joy lay a covert demand for peace at
any price. Its other principal theme is paradise. As for the reason
why this idea featured concurrently with that of Ocean in Coleridge's reading and notes, I believe it to have been the primary and
radical connection we have observed between the ideal enclave and
the sea.

Interest in the origins of *The Ancient Mariner* has gathered momentum among Coleridge's readers ever since Lowes, in *The Road to Xanadu*, established by following scattered clues in the Note Book a large number of verbal correspondences between the poem and words or phrases in books which had recently featured in Coleridge's omnivorous reading. But Lowes's analysis also caused frustration and disquiet. Where was the organizing principle within this seemingly adventitious mass of reading? And what process of sublimation could suddenly have elicited so taut and coherent a poem from such inchoate material? Lowes's explanation in terms of 'the hooks and eyes of memory' seemed in this respect gravely deficient; yet there was virtually no hard evidence by which to counter the formidable body of information he had adduced to support his view of the poem's genesis. The Note Book has since come to be regarded as rather unpromising material for further investigation, partly owing to its discursive character, but also because of the seemingly exhaustive treatment accorded to it in *The Road to Xanadu*. This was certainly the view I had myself taken, until, seeking to confirm that *The Ancient Mariner* is the product and expression of a divided imagination, I came—at the beginning of a passage notable, as I hope to show presently, for the sense it gives of an imagination at odds with itself—upon the following entry (*C.N.* 53):

> Νὴ τὸν Δί᾽ ἔγωγ᾽ οὖν "Ονος ἄγων μυστήρια.
> Ἀτὰρ οὐ καθέξω ταῦτα τὸν πλείω χρόνον.
>
> *Arist. Βατραι.*

(I'm the donkey participating in the mysteries but I'll not endure these things an instant longer. Aristophanes: *The Frogs*.)

The immediately preceding lines in *The Frogs* consist of a discussion between Dionysus and Heracles about the former's intended voyage across the Acherusian Lake to the Underworld, so that he may find the shade of Euripides, because there is no true poet left in the world:

HERACLES.   A parlous voyage that,
    For first you'll come to an enormous lake
    Of fathomless depth.

DIONYSUS.   And how am I to cross?
HERACLES. An ancient mariner will row you over
In a wee boat, *so* big. The fare's two obols.
DIONYSUS. Fie! The power two obols have, the whole world
    through!
How came they thither!
HERACLES.   Theseus took them down.
And next you'll see great snakes and savage monsters
In tens of thousands.
DIONYSUS.   You needn't try to scare me,
I'm going to go.
HERACLES.   Then weltering seas of filth
And ever-rippling dung: and plunged therein,
Whoso has wronged the stranger here on earth.
        [6 lines on comparable offenders]
And next the breath of flutes will float around you,
And glorious sunshine, such as ours, you'll see,
And myrtle groves, and happy bands who clap
Their hands in triumph, men and women too.
DIONYSUS. And who are they?
HERACLES.   The happy mystic bands.

I give the passage in B. B. Rogers's translation because, although
he may well have been influenced by Coleridge in choosing the
phrase 'an ancient mariner', it does justice to Aristophanes' words,
γέρων ναύτης (an old sailor), which most other versions do not.

The importance of the Aristophanes passage as a source is unlikely to be disputed. Nowhere else in Coleridge's known reading
appears a group of the poem's main ideas in an order approximating
to their place in its thought-sequence. It has plainly influenced the
dense sea on which the ship rides idle and motionless:

> The very deep did rot: O Christ!
> That ever this should be!
> Yea, slimy things did crawl with legs
> Upon the slimy sea.

It must have supplied the all-important water-snakes, hitherto
poorly served, apart from incidental detail, by suggested sources.

And it has unmistakably contributed the strange musical sounds (even the main instrument) which are suddenly heard in Part V:

> And now 'twas like all instruments,
> Now like a lonely flute;
> And now it is an angel's song,
> That makes the heavens be mute.

Moreover, the sudden intervention of pastoral imagery in the same section, as well as the Hermit's 'wood / Which slopes down to the sea', are clearly indebted to its myrtle groves. Perhaps most important of all, Coleridge's use of this source indicates that the figure on whom he based the Mariner was not the traditional Wandering Jew, with whom he is known to have associated him, but Charon, and that the story which provided the schema of his poem told of a voyage to the Underworld. All this affects our view of the poem's conception and development: it tells against the improbable theory that Coleridge was jockeyed from association to association until scattered particles from his immense reading were fused by a mysterious alchemy, for it shows that many of the basic ideas assembled in *The Ancient Mariner* had never been disjoined in the first place.

Coleridge's Letters reveal his strong admiration for the plays of Aristophanes. On 2 July 1816 Coleridge writes to his friend John Hookham Frere, whose volume of Aristophanes translations he valued sufficiently to make his copy of it a separate item in his will:

and I say less than I mean & feel, when I add that I have on my shelves long original poems, epic, and romantic, full of images and incidents and *mother-and-child* Sentiments and sensibilities, and these of great celebrity, (*reputation* at least) the whole excellences of which concentrated do not impress on my reason that sense of inventive and constructive power, which I appeared to myself to see in the one Imitation of the Parabasis from the Knights of Aristophanes.[1]

But the most telling evidence for his deep and sustained feeling for *The Frogs* occurs in his letter to Wordsworth of 30 May 1815, in

---

[1] *C.L.* iv. 647.

which he distils his recollection of his excitement on first reading
The Prelude in a single Greek sentence, με | αὖρα τις εἰσέπνευσε
μυστικωτάτη. (There breathed on me a most mystical breeze.) It
comes from the same part of *The Frogs* (l. 314) as the lines we have
been considering.

In Aristophanes' play, the frogs whose chorus accompanies and
exasperates Dionysus on his voyage are, of course, acutely poetic
creatures, loved by the Muses, as well as by Pan and Apollo, for
their 'myriad-diving roundelays'; yet it could be much too lightly
assumed that Coleridge, even though he drew on this comedy as
a literary source for his greatest poem, must surely have remained
indifferent or unattuned to live frogs themselves, the lowly amphi-
bians in which the great Attic comedian took unashamed delight
and found inspiration: but there is evidence that suggests otherwise.
In October 1804 Coleridge enters in his Note Book for that period
(*C.N.* 2212),

> Went on shore to cross to Tremilla / observed what I concluded to
> be the green bulb or tumour of a rush / Yet why did I look again?—
> The understanding of the obscure feelings. It was a green frog stick-
> ing to the Stalk like an old Bigot at his prayers—His Hands up, & his
> under jaw membrane trembling half bladder-motion, half life—What
> (?quantity)—how striking yet (?bugbear)

What principle, he asks, alerted and piloted his attention, when
sense-perception alone would presumably have missed the incon-
spicuous and perfectly camouflaged creature. 'The understanding
of the obscure feelings': it is not much of an answer, at best delimit-
ing the area where an explanation should be sought, at worst
representable as only an empty phrase standing in for the lack of
one. But the flash of understanding which leads Coleridge to ask the
question is typical of genius; and over the issue at stake here, the
decisive importance of such matters as noticing, or failing to notice,
a particular frog on a particular day, the thought of Coleridge and
Blake, in many ways so divergent, momentarily coincides against
that of lesser minds.

Throughout the Note Book, as we have said, Coleridge constantly reverts to the idea of Ocean, which features both in its literal and its mythological aspects. On page forty-nine he writes (*C.N.* 246-7),

Water

Ὠκεανόν τε γὰρ καὶ Τηθὺν ἐποίησαν τῆς γενέσεως πατέρας, καὶ τὸν ὅρκον τῶν θεῶν ὕδωρ, τὴν καλουμένην ὑπ' αὐτῶν Στύγα τῶν ποιητῶν. τιμιώτατον μὲν γὰρ τὸ πρεσβύτατον, ὅρκος δὲ τὸ τιμιώτατόν ἐστιν.[1]

Arist. *Metaph.* I. i.c. 3

Ὠκεανόν τε θεῶν γένεσιν καὶ μητέρα Τηθύν.[2]

And on another page he writes (*C.N.* 213),

> The swallows interweaving there mid the paired
> Sea-mews,[3] at distance wildly-wailing.—
> The brook runs over Sea-weeds,—

It seems certain that Coleridge was well aware of the poet's assignment with the primordial element, and also of the relevance of the idea of Ocean to Blake's question, 'Who shall bind the Infinite?', for otherwise he would not have written (*C.N.* 273),

> great things that on the ocean
> counterfeit infinity—

He was evidently aware too that our notion of an ideal enclave is fundamentally related to the motif of Ocean. The Note Book leaves little doubt that the idea of paradise converged in Coleridge's mind with that of Ocean to form a single matrix of thought and imaginative ferment. Paradise provides, as we have already observed, its

---

[1] Ocean and Tethys are held to have been the origin: and for this cause the oath of the Gods is said to be by water (called by the poets Styx) as being that from which they all derived their original. For an oath ought to be by that which is most honourable; and that which is most ancient is most honourable.

[2] Ocean, the origin of the gods and Tethys their mother.

[3] The sea-mews are in themselves suggestive, for Coleridge's well-known general penchant for Neoplatonic daemons does not fully explain why the idea of shooting an albatross, put forward by Wordsworth, was accepted by him: we need to account for the exact poetic appropriateness of such a sea-bird. And it will be remembered that Homer, needing a sufficient image for Mercury on a trans-oceanic errand, chose the sea-mew, 'drenching the feathers of its wings with spray as it pursues the fish down desolate gulfs of the unharvested deep'.

second main theme. On page twenty-eight Coleridge notes (*C.N.* 191),

> In the paradisiacal World Sleep was voluntary & holy—a spiritual before God, in which the mind elevated by contemplation retired into pure intellect suspending all commerce with sensible objects & perceiving the present deity—

On page thirty-two he sets down (*C.N.* 220),

> Some wilderness-plot, green and fountainous and unviolated by Man.

There are also, of course, the evidences of reading associated with this idea from such works as Burnet's *Sacred Theory* traced in *The Road to Xanadu*. And in the passage which precedes the key entry from *The Frogs* it is directly connected with the sea in a reference to Sicily, rich in paradisial associations (*C.N.* 51):

> Light cargoes waft of modulated Sound
> From viewless Hybla brought, when Melodies
> Like Birds of Paradise on wings, that aye
> Disport in wild variety of hues,
> Murmur around the honey-dropping flowers.

Coleridge's persisting responsiveness to meadows and pastoral landscape running down to the sea's edge and the significance he attached to them are further shown by an entry in the 1802 Note Book (*C.N.* 1227):

> I now pass on, beyond the source of the hither Beck, to the top of the Hill along which & up which my road had been ever winding, & see behind me to my right a grand Seaview & the flat lands upon the Sea, with 3 Hills, the largest of which looks like a Paradise in the wild, the fields so sweetly shaped & so green, the smaller is not unlike it, the hither one is bleak/

Yet, irresistibly though the idea of Ocean attracts Coleridge, it also excites in him intense fear. The couplet from *The Frogs* about the mutinous donkey in the mystery-show is important in itself for our understanding of Coleridge, and of the ambivalence of feeling that divided his imagination, and must be considered in the context of the entries that follow it:

> The Whale followed by *Waves*—I would glide down the rivulet of quiet Life, a Trout!
>> Broad-breasted Rock.
>> hanging cliff that glasses
>> His rugged forehead in the calmy sea.

—Bad means for a good end—I cannot conceive that (there can be) any road to Heaven through Hell—

Coleridge, surely, omits the crucial material, the old sailor and the voyage to the Underworld, out of a palpable resistance towards it, expressed by his retention of one idea only: enduring the mysteries and serving as their pack-animal no longer. He then rationalizes his fear of primordial Ocean, his longing to escape from it and to glide quiescently like a trout, by pretending that no road to Heaven can lead through Hell. In the Note Book we see him again and again recoiling from the idea of the sea towards images of enveloping torpor. The idea of a sea-voyage, a favourite theme of Coleridge, is followed by a vignette of a child being lulled to sleep (*C.N.* 225, 226):

> An abrupt beginning followed by an even & majestic greatness compared to the Launching of a Ship, which after sails on in a steady breeze.—

> The Infant playing with its mother's Shadow—Rocking its little sister's cradle & singing to her with inarticulate voice.—

Sleep at sea is also idealized in a sequence of thoughts on the apotheosis of man (*C.N.* 20–23):

> When lulled Reason sleeps on the stormy Bosom of
> Transport, as a ship boy in the Shrouds—
>> [4 lines on Optimism and Love]
> This is the true Sublime of Man! this the Meridian
> Majesty of our Nature!

And yet we must assume it to have been part of Coleridge's tragedy that, at some unspecifiable level of awareness, he knew all this to be self-delusion, for only thus can we make sense of such entries as (*C.N.* 272):

> unbind the poppy garland—

and (*C.N.* 273):

> Why sleep ye, O ye Watchman—
> Wake from the sleep of whoredom. trim your Lamp—
> Sound, sound the Trumpets—for the Bridegroom comes—
> O man, thou half-dead Angel—

This whole pattern of thought and feeling is profoundly consonant with Coleridge's critically important letter of 14 October 1797 to John Thelwall in which he writes,

> I should much wish, like the Indian Vishnu, to float about along an infinite ocean cradled in the flower of the Lotos, and wake once in a million years for a few minutes—just to know that I was going to sleep a million years more.[1]

He then quotes a passage from *Osorio* which includes the lines

> O would to Alla,
> The Raven and the Seamew were appointed
> To bring me food—or rather that my Soul
> Could drink in life from the universal air!
> It were a lot divine in some small skiff
> Along some Ocean's boundless solitude
> To float for ever with a careless course,
> And think myself the only Being alive!

Surely here is the heart of the matter: no one can afford to think of embarking on that ocean with the flower of the lotus as his skiff, or, contemplating that passage, to make any concession at all to the enchantment of oblivion.

The Note Book confirms that Coleridge was unequal to the ultimate task of the poet, which is to bring together those dimensions of the mind whose dissociation in Coleridge's case is so powerfully and exactly realized in *The Ancient Mariner*. At heart he was an

[1] *C.L.* i. 350.

inhabitant of the earthly paradise. And the earthly paradise is insufficient for man, because it is incapable of uniting the opposed ideals symbolized by snake and tree, the world of Cleopatra and that of *The Winter's Tale*, Mariner and Wedding Guest. Over against it, as we have seen, stands a more severe paradisial myth, over-shadowing pleasure-fantasies, arcadias, and all such lesser ideal forms, reaching back to the unknown first time when the snake-encircled tree was incorporated in the ideal enclave, not as earthly elysium but as divine precinct, to set forth a reconciliation of these divergent human ends, and the power of imagination by which it may be accomplished. As embodying this unitive power, Sumerians and Greeks assigned the image in miniature to the figure who represented for them, as he can for us, the function of the mind that mediates between ourselves and the forces within us to which we give the name of gods. The strength of the underlying symbolic principle further manifests itself, I believe, in the snake-encircled tree as it appears on the Greek hero-reliefs, treated as an object of veneration and a source of bounty. And, as I have tried to show, this principle unfolds itself, and assumes yet subtler forms, in Shakespeare's last plays, in Giorgione's great masterpiece, and, superimposed on a largely alien story, in *Paradise Lost*. Although the alternative myth realized in these poetic structures does not offer peace or reassurance, it is yet necessary and profoundly satisfying; for it is central to that imaginative life which sets before us and reconciles the contrary modes of fulfilment we seek: to frequent the region of the infinitely various, to stand rooted in a continuing order. But Coleridge shows we must not confront it half asleep, or hope to grasp it unscathed.

INDEX

Abu Shahrein, 10.
Acherusian Lake, 139.
Achilles, 24.
Acropolis, the, 30, 31.
Adam, 14, 21, 110–12, 115, 118–20.
Adapa, 13–14, 22.
Aea, 19.
Aeetes, King, 19.
Aegle, 18.
Aesacus, 99.
Aeschylus, 12.
Agelaus, 99.
Akkad, 9.
Alciati, 67.
Alcinous, 106.
Alcuin, 114.
Alexandria, 56.
Allsop, T., cited, 132.
Ancestor-figures, 26–8, 67.
Antony, Mark, 44–60.
Anu, 11, 14–15, 22.
Aphrodite, 48; *see also* Venus.
Apollo, 23, 30–1, 62, 71, 142.
Apollodorus, 17–18, 30, 99, 105.
Apollonius Rhodius, 17, 19–20, 83.
Apples, golden, 17–19.
Apsu, 9, 10.
Araxes, 19.
Arcadia, Arcadians, 23, 67, 147.
Ares, 20, 30.
Arethusa, 18.
Argonauts, voyage of the, 19–20.
Aristophanes, 139–42, 144.
Aristotle, 143.
Artemis, 31.
Arthur, King, 95.
Asklepios, snake-staff of, 22.
Athena, 67, 100; sacred animal of, 30.
Athens, founder, 30, 67.
Atlas, 17, 18.
Atrahasis fragment, 11.
Augeas, 18.
Augustine, 112, 114.
Autolycus, 71.

Babylonian, literature, 9–14, 23, 89, 117;
   myths, 13–14, 71; sacred tree, 10, 32.

Ballad of Sir Patrick Spens, 130.
Baptism, Order of, 89.
Bellini, G., *Sacred Allegory*, 101–2.
Benivieni's *Amore*, 42.
Blake, William, 5, 7, 43, 50, 105, 122,
   130–3, 142–3.
Boccaccio, 39, 42, 100.
Boreas, 41.
Botticelli, *Primavera*, 23, 39–43, 60, 103,
   107; *The Birth of Venus*, 47.
Braunfels, W., cited, 102.
Burnet, Thomas, 144.

Cadmus, 30.
Caduceus (snake-staff), 21–5, 40, 43, 103.
Calypso, 24.
Catullus, 109.
Cecrops, 30, 67.
Cerberus, 27.
Ceres, 90.
Ceto, 17.
Charon, 141.
Children, abandoned, 66–7, 99–102;
   association between child and snake,
   53–4, 66–7, 102; hurtfulness, 81.
Chittenden, J., cited, 25.
Chloris, transformation into Flora (q.v.),
   40–1.
Christianity, 21, 123.
Chthonian powers, 27, 31, 33–4, 76.
Clark, Sir Kenneth, quoted, 98–9.
Cleopatra, 44–60, 68, 137, 146.
Colchis, 19.
Coleridge, George, 132.
Coleridge, Samuel Taylor, 4, 43–4; *The
   Ancient Mariner*, 84, 124–34, 136–47;
   Dejection Ode, 130, 136; *Kubla Khan*,
   110, 124, 134–8; Letters, 131–3, 141,
   146; Note Books, 130, 138–9, 142–6.
Cologne *Paradise Garden*, 103.
Cosimo, Piero di, 83.
Cronos, 23, 70.
Cross, the, 21.
Cupid, 40, 46–7.
Cyllene, 23, 24.
Cyprus, 47.
Cythera, 47.

Dante, 69, 82.
Delos, 31.
Delphos, 62.
Demeter, 70, 109.
De Waele, J. W. M., cited, 23.
Dilmun, land of, 10.
Dionysus, 29, 139–40, 142.
Dioscuri, 67.
Dodds, E. R., cited, 12.
Dodona, 31.
Dogs, on hero-reliefs, 27, 29; on sea shore, 82–3; spirits in the shape of, 92.
Dreams, 112.
Dupuis, 125.
Dürer, Albrecht, 83.

Echidna, 18.
Eleans, 67.
Eliot, T. S., *Four Quartets*, 137; *The Waste Land*, 88.
Elis, 67.
Enki (water-god), 10, 16, 22.
Enkidu, 16–17, 79.
Enlil, 11, 15.
Erasmus, 84.
Erechtheus, 31, 41, 67.
Eridu, 10.
Erythia, 18.
Euphrates, 8, 15.
Euripides, 17–18, 139.
Eurystheus, 17, 18.
Evans, M., cited, 114.
Eve, 3–4, 109–20.
Evolution, concept of, 3.

Fall of Man, story of the, Genesis story, 3–4, 6, 9–15, 118; Milton's treatment of, 114–23.
Farnell, L. R., cited, 31.
Fertility symbols, 32–3.
Flood, story of the, 11–14.
Flora, 40–41, 60, 68.
Flower-goddess, 40, 68.
Flowers, gathering, 69–70, 109; in Milton, 119; in *Primavera*, 41; maiden as flower, 109.
Frankfort, Henri, cited, 6, 22.
Frere, John Hookham, 141.
Frogs, 142.
Frothingham, A. L., cited, 22.
Furtwängler, cited, 27.

Gardens, image of, 109–10.
Garin, E., cited, 34.
Garrod, Professor H. W., cited, 134.
Genesis story, 3–4, 6, 9–15, 118.
Gilgamesh Epic, 9, 12–14, 16, 48, 79, 117–18.
Giorgione, *La Tempesta*, 98–103, 106, 121, 147; *The Finding of Paris*, 99–100.
Giraldi, 39.
Gizzida, 22.
Golden apples, 17–19.
Golden Fleece, 19–20, 94.
Golding, A., cited, 69, 93.
Gombrich, E. H., cited, 34.
Graces, 23, 40–2, 103.
Gravestones, Greek; *see* Greek hero-reliefs.
Greek hero-reliefs, 25–36, 147.
Greek myth, 4, 17–20, 25, 104, 147; visual imagery, 22–3, 25.
Greek religion, 26, 29, 30; tree-syndrome, 31.
Greene, Robert, *Pandosto*, 61, 71, 73.
Griggs, E. L., cited, 134.
Gudea, 21–2.
Guillaume de Deguilleville, 102.

Hades, 24, 26, 27.
Harpies, 83–4.
Harrison, Jane, cited, 29–30, 33–4.
Hazlitt, William, 134.
Hecate, 27.
Hecuba, 99.
Held, Julius S., cited, 60.
Hera, 17, 18, 23; *see also* Juno.
Heracles, 9, 17, 18, 31, 56–7, 139–40.
Herbert, George, quoted, 79.
Hercules; *see* Heracles.
Hermes, 23–5; snake-staff of, 22–4; *see also* Mercury.
Hero-reliefs, Greek, 25–36, 147.
Herodotus, 28, 30, 31.
Heroes, 56–8.
Hesiod, 17, 48, 83, 105.
Hesperia, 18.
Hesperides myth, 17–19, 102, 104–6, 121.
Homer, 9, 12–14, 19, 24–6, 106, 143.
Homeric *Hymn to Demeter*, 70, 109.
Homeric *Hymn to Hermes*, 23, 72.
Horses, on hero-reliefs, 27, 29.
House, Humphry, cited, 130.
Housman, A. E., 137.

Huluppu-Tree, 15–17, 48.
Hyperboreans, 18.

Iapetus, 18.
Ida, Mount, 99.
Imagination, 77, 96, 131–9, 147.
Immortality, 9, 13–14, 114, 117–18.
Inanna (Ishtar), 12, 15–17, 104.
Ion, 67.
Iris (goddess), 54, 90.
Ishtar; *see* Inanna.

Jason, 19, 20, 93–4.
Jealousy, Castle of, 63–4.
Jews, 5, 141.
Johansen, K. Fr., cited, 26.
Juno, 90, 100; *see also* Hera.

Keats, John, 133.
Kermode, J. F., cited, 78, 118.
Kiškanu-tree, 10.
Kott, Jan, cited, 60.
Kramer, S. N., cited, 8–10, 15, 36.
Kristeller, P. O., cited, 34.

Ladner, G. B., cited, 76.
Lagash, 21.
Landscape in Renaissance art, 39 ff.
La Rochefoucauld, F., 52.
Laurels, 31, 35.
Leavis, F. R., cited, 76, 121–2.
Leto, 31.
Lilith, 16.
Lowes, J. L., cited, 125, 138–9, 144.
Ludwig, cited, 102.
Lycus, 19.

Macrobius, 112.
Maia, 23.
Marathon, Battle of, 28.
May-pole and may-tree, 21.
Medea, 19–20, 93–4.
Meidias painter, 18.
Meiss, E., cited, 60, 76.
Mercury, 71, 82, 84, 100, 107, 128, 143;
    role in *Primavera*, 40–3, 103, 107;
    snake-staff of, 40, 43, 103; *see also*
    Hermes.
Merops, 99.
Metamorphosis, 82–3, 88–9, 108.

Michiel, M., 98.
Milan, Duchy of, 67.
Milton, John, *Comus*, 104–6, 121;
    Paradise Lost, 4, 66, 104–23, 147;
    status as poet, 121–3.
Minoan–Mycenaean religion, 30–2.
Mirandola, Pico della; *see* Pico della
    Mirandola.
Moon, references to the, 46, 129–30.
Morelli, G., cited, 101.
Moses, 67; rod, 21.
Mummu, 9.
Music, 88.
'Myth' (word), 5.

Nammu, 10.
Narcissus, 70, 109.
Neoplatonists, 5, 34–5, 40, 42, 102,
    125, 143.
New Testament, 88.
Nilsson, M. P., cited, 28, 30–1, 67.
Ningizzida, god, 21–2, 25.
Ninhursag, 10.
Nippur, 6, 11.
North, Sir Thomas, 46.
Nymphs, 23, 90.

Ocean, 10, 137–8, 143–6.
Ogygia island, 24.
Olympia, 31.
Ovid, 18, 20, 40–1, 68–9, 93–4, 105,
    109.

Pan, 142.
'Paradise' (word), 3.
Paradise Lost; see under Milton, John.
Paris, Finding of, 99–100.
Pater, Walter, 98.
Pausanias, 67.
Pergamon, relief from, 29.
Perrot, N., cited, 11, 31–2.
Persephone, 26, 70, 73, 108–9; *see also*
    Proserpina.
Perseus, 18.
Persians, 28, 31.
Phasis, 19.
Pherekydes, 17.
Phorcys, 17.
Pico della Mirandola, 34, 40, 42.
Piraeus, relief from, 29.
Plutarch, 28, 46, 48, 55–6, 60.

Pluto, 70.
Priam, 24, 99.
Primavera; see Botticelli.
Prometheus, 71.
Proserpina, 69, 109; *see also* Persephone.
Python, 30.

Quattrocento, 39.

Raphael, 83.
Rasmo, N., cited, 102
Reik, T., cited, 4.
Remus, 67.
Reynolds, Sir Joshua, quoted, 133.
Richter, G. M., cited, 100.
Rilke, R. M., quoted, 26, 48, 96–7.
Rogers, B. B., cited, 140.
Roman de la Rose MS., 63.
Romulus, 67.

Salamis, Battle of, 28.
Samos, relief from, 29.
Samuqan, god of cattle, 79.
Satan, 106–17, 120–1, 123.
Sea, the (*see also* Ocean), 9–10.
Sea-mews, 143, 146.
Sea-nymphs, 82, 88.
Serpent; *see* Snake.
Seznec, Jean, cited, 39–40.
Shakespeare, *Antony and Cleopatra*, 43–60,
  65, 75–6, 88, 96, 129; *Coriolanus*,
  60; final period, 4, 39, 43–97, 100,
  147; *King Lear*, 78, 123; *A Midsummer Night's Dream*, 77, 93; Milton
  and, 121–2; *The Tempest*, 43, 77–97,
  101–3, 106, 121; *The Winter's Tale*,
  43, 60–77, 85, 90, 96, 103, 107–9,
  137, 146.
Smith Cylinder (British Museum), 11.
Snake: association between child and
  snake, 53–4, 66–7, 102; Cleopatra
  and, 53–5; 'serpent of old Nile', 48,
  54; significance, 30–6, 48, 103, 116,
  146–7; snake-encircled tree, 15–36,
  77, 86, 94, 101, 104–5, 121, 137–8,
  146–7; water-snakes, 127, 137, 140.
Snake-goddess, 30.
Snake-staff (or caduceus), 21–5, 40, 43,
  103.
Sophocles, 12.
Sosipolis, 67.
Spenser, Edmund, 103.

Spring, Eternal, 69, 108–9; theme, 40–1,
  69.
Spurgeon, Miss, 65.
Stewart, J. I. M., cited, 61.
Sumerian myth, 4, 6, 8–17, 21–2, 25,
  48, 71, 79, 104–5, 147.
Sun-God, 10, 16.
Symbols, 34–5.

Tammuz, 22.
Tempesta, La; see Giorgione.
Teniers, 99.
Tethys, 143.
Thebans, 30.
Theft, poetic value of, 71–3, 107–8.
Thelwall, John, 132, 146.
Themis of Parnassus, 18.
Themistocles, 28.
Theocritus, 103.
Theseus, 28, 140.
Thieves, 40, 71–3, 103, 107–8, 110.
Thyrean relief, 29.
Tiamat, 9.
Tigris, 8.
Toscanne, P., cited, 11.
Tree, in Greek religious thought, 31;
  characteristics, 76–7; significance, 30–
  5; snake-encircled tree; *see under*
  Snake.
Tree-branch sceptre; *see* Caduceus.
Tree of Knowledge, 114.
Tree of Life, 10, 76, 116–17.
Trilling, Lionel, quoted, 4.
Tuve, Rosemond, 105.
Typhon, 18.

Ulysses, 24, 71.
Underworld, 16–17, 22–8, 139, 141,
  145.
Ur, 22.
Urshanabi, 13.
Uruk, 15.
Utnapishtim, 13.
Utu (sun-god), 16.

van Buren, E. D., cited, 22.
Vasari, G., cited, 40.
Vase-paintings, 18–19, 21, 30, 64.
Venus, 40–1, 46–8, 63, 100.
Virgil, 100, 103.

Wandering Jew, 141.
Water, metamorphosis by, 88–9; as primordial element, 9–10, 88–9.
Water-God, 10, 16, 22.
Water-snakes, 127, 137, 140.
Widengren, G., cited, 10.
Wind, E., cited, 40–3.
Wordsworth, William, 71–3, 130, 133, 141, 143.

Yahweh, 12.
Yeats, W. B., 35.

Zephyr, 40–2.
Zeus, 17–18, 23–4, 30–1, 70–1, 109.
Zu, Babylonian myth, 71.
Zu-bird, 15, 16.

PRINTED IN GREAT BRITAIN
AT THE UNIVERSITY PRESS, OXFORD
BY VIVIAN RIDLER
PRINTER TO THE UNIVERSITY